Harrison Weir

**Favourite Fables**

In Prose and Verse

Harrison Weir

**Favourite Fables**
*In Prose and Verse*

ISBN/EAN: 9783744689366

Printed in Europe, USA, Canada, Australia, Japan

Cover: Foto ©Thomas Meinert / pixelio.de

More available books at **www.hansebooks.com**

# FAVOURITE FABLES,

## In Prose and Verse.

## With Twenty-four Illustrations

### FROM DRAWINGS

## By Harrison Weir.

JUSTICE.

LONDON
GRIFFITH AND FARRAN,
(SUCCESSORS TO NEWBERY AND HARRIS),
CORNER OF ST. PAUL'S CHURCHYARD.
MDCCCLXX.

# CONTENTS.

iv CONTENTS.

VI                          CONTENTS.

# FAVOURITE FABLES.

## FABLE I.

### THE FOX AND THE GOAT.

N the extreme end of a village a Fox one day went to have a peep at a hen-roost. He had the bad luck to fall into a well, where he swam first to this side, and then to that side, but could not get out with all his pains. At last, as chance would have it, a poor Goat came to the same place to seek for some drink. "So ho! friend Fox," said he, "you quaff it off there at a great rate: I hope by this time you have quenched your thirst." "Thirst!" said the sly rogue; "what I have found here to drink is so clear, and so sweet, that I cannot take my fill of it; do, pray, come down, my dear, and have a taste of it." With that, in plumped the Goat as he bade him; but as soon as he was down, the Fox jumped on his horns, and leaped out of the well in a trice; and as he went off, "Good bye, my wise friend," said he; "if you had as much brains as you have beard, I should have been in the well still, and you might have stood on the brink of it to laugh at me, as I now do at you."

MORAL.

A rogue will give up the best friend he has to get out of a scrape; so that we ought to know what a man is, that we may judge how far we may trust to what he says.

————

## FABLE II.

### THE FROG AND THE OX.

An old Frog, being wonderfully struck with the size and majesty of an Ox that was grazing in the marshes, was seized with the desire to expand herself to the same portly magnitude. After puffing and swelling for some time, "What think you," said she, to her young ones, "will this do?" "Far from it," said they. "Will this?" "By no means." " But this surely will ?" " Nothing like it," they replied. After many fruitless and ridiculous efforts to the same purpose, the foolish Frog burst her skin, and miserably expired upon the spot.

### MORAL.

To attempt what is out of our power, and to rival those greater than ourselves, is sure to expose us to contempt and ruin.

———o———

## FABLE III.

### THE MAN AND HIS GOOSE.

A CERTAIN Man had a Goose, which laid him a golden egg every day. But, not contented with this, which rather increased than abated his avarice, he was resolved to kill the Goose, and cut up her belly, so that he might come to the inexhaustible treasure which he fancied she had within her, without being obliged to wait for the slow production of a single egg daily. He did so, and, to his great sorrow and disappointment, found nothing within.

### MORAL.

The man that hastes to become rich often finds that he has only brought on ruin.

## FABLE IV.

### THE LION AND OTHER BEASTS.

THE Bull, and several other beasts, were ambitious of the honour of hunting with the Lion. His savage Majesty graciously condescended to their desire; and it was agreed that they should have an equal share in whatever might be taken. They scour the forest, are unanimous in the pursuit and, after a long chase, pull down a noble stag. It was divided with great dexterity by the Bull into four equal parts; but just as he was going to secure his share— "Hold!" says the Lion, "let no one presume to help himself till he hath heard our just and reasonable claims. I seize upon the first quarter by virtue of my prerogative; the second I claim as due to my superior conduct and courage I cannot forego the third, on account of the necessities of my den; and if anyone is inclined to dispute my right to the fourth, let him speak." Awed by the majesty of his frown and the terror of his paws, they silently withdrew, resolving never to hunt again but with their equals.

### MORAL.

Be certain that those who have great power are honest before you place yourselves in their hands, or you will be deprived of your just rights.

## FABLE V.

### THE DOVE AND THE ANT.

THE Ant, compelled by thirst, went to drink in a clear, purling rivulet; but the current, with its circling eddy, snatched her away, and carried her down the stream. A Dove, pitying her distressed condition, cropped a branch from a neighbouring tree and let it fall into the water, by means of which the Ant saved herself and got ashore. Not long after, a Fowler, having a design against the Dove, planted his nets in due order, without the bird's observing what he was about; which the Ant perceiving, just as he was going to put his design into execution, she bit his heel, and made him give so sudden a start, that the Dove took the alarm, and flew away.

#### MORAL.

Kindness to others seldom fails of its reward; and none is so weak that he may not be able in some fashion to repay it. Let us show kindness without looking for a return, but a blessing will surely follow.

## FABLE VI.

### THE FOX WITHOUT A TAIL.

A Fox being caught in a steel trap by his tail, was glad to compound for his escape with the loss of it; but on coming abroad into the world, began to be so sensible of the disgrace such a defect would bring upon him, that he almost wished he had died rather than left it behind him. However, to make the best of a bad matter, he formed a project in his head to call an assembly of the rest of the Foxes, and propose it for their imitation as a fashion which would be very agreeable and becoming. He did so, and made a long harangue upon the unprofitableness of tails in general, and endeavoured chiefly to show the awkwardness and inconvenience of a Fox's tail in particular; adding that it would be both more graceful and more expeditious to be altogether without them, and that, for his part, what he had only imagined and conjectured before, he now found by experience; for that he never enjoyed himself so well, nor found himself so easy as he had done since he cut off his tail. He said no more, but looked about with a brisk air to see what proselytes he had gained; when a sly old Fox in the company, who understood trap, answered

THE FOX WITHOUT A TAIL.

him, with a leer, "I believe you may have found a con-
veniency in parting with your tail; and when we are in the
same circumstances, perhaps we may do so too."

### MORAL.

It is common for men to wish others reduced to their own
level, and we ought to guard against such advice as may
proceed from this principle.

——o——

## FABLE VII.

### THE BUTTERFLY AND THE SNAIL.

As in the sunshine of the morn,
A Butterfly, but newly born,
Sat proudly perking on a rose,
With pert conceit his bosom glows;
His wings, all glorious to behold,
Bedropt with azure, jet and gold,
Wide he displays; the spangled dew
Reflects his eyes, and various hue.

His now forgotten friend, a Snail,
Beneath his house, with slimy trail,
Crawls o'er the grass; whom, when he spies,
In wrath he to the gardener cries:

" What means yon peasant's daily toil,
From choaking weeds to rid the soil?
Why wake you to the morning's care?
Why with new arts correct the year?
Why glows the peach with crimson hue?
And why the plum's inviting blue?
Were they to feast his taste designed,
That vermin, of voracious kind?
Crush, then, the slow, the pilf'ring race;
So purge thy garden from disgrace."

"What arrogance!" the Snail replied;
"How insolent is upstart pride!
Hadst thou not thus, with insult vain,
Provoked my patience to complain,
I had concealed thy meaner birth,
Nor traced thee to the scum of earth:
For, scarce nine suns have wak'd the hours,
To swell the fruit, and paint the flowers,
Since I thy humbler life surveyed,
In base, in sordid guise arrayed;
A hideous insect, vile, unclean,
You dragg'd a slow and noisome train;
And from your spider-bowels drew
Foul film, and spun the dirty clue.

I own my humble life, good friend;
Snail was I born, and Snail shall end.
And what's a Butterfly?   At best,
He's but a Caterpillar, dress'd;
And all thy race (a numerous seed)
Shall prove of Caterpillar breed."

### MORAL.

All upstarts, insolent in place,
Remind us of their vulgar race.

———o———

## FABLE VIII.

### THE WOLF AND THE CRANE.

A WOLF, after too greedily devouring his prey, happened
to have a bone stick in his throat, which gave him so much
pain that he went howling up and down, and importuning
every creature he met to lend him a kind hand in order to
his relief; nay, he even promised a reward to anyone who
should undertake the operation with success.   At last the
Crane, tempted with the lucre of the reward, and having first
made the Wolf confirm his promise with an oath, undertook
the business, and ventured his long neck into the rapacious
felon's throat.

In short, he plucked out the bone, and expected the promised gratuity; when the Wolf, turning his eyes disdainfully

towards him, said, "I did not think you had been so un-reasonable! Have I not suffered you safely to draw your neck out of my jaws? And have you the conscience to demand a further reward?"

MORAL.

When we do good to bad men, we must not expect good from them.

——◦——

FABLE IX.

THE FROG AND THE RAT.

ONCE on a time, a foolish Frog,
Vain, proud, and stupid as a log,
Tired with the marsh, her native home,
Imprudently abroad would roam,
And fix her habitation where
She'd breathe at least a purer air.
She was resolved to change, that's poz;
Could she be worse than where she was?

Away the silly creature leaps.
A Rat, who saw her lab'ring steps,
Cried out, "Where in this hurry, pray?
You certainly will go astray!"

" Ne'er fear; I quit that filthy bog,
Where I so long have croaked incog:
People of talents, sure, should thrive,
And not be buried thus alive.
But, pray (for I'm extremely dry),
Know you of any water nigh?"

" None," said the Rat, "you'll reach to-day,
As you so slowly make your way.
Believe a friend, and take my word,
This jaunt of yours is quite absurd.
Go to your froggery again;
In your own element remain."
No: on the journey she was bent,
Her thirst increasing as she went;
For want of drink she scarce can hop,
And yet despairing of a drop:
Too late she moans her folly past;
She faints, she sinks, she breathes her last.

MORAL.

Vulgar minds will pay full dear,
When once they move beyond their sphere.

# FABLE X.

## THE FIGHTING COCK AND EAGLE.

Two Cocks were fighting for the sovereignty of the dung-hill, and one of them having got the better of the other, he that was vanquished crept into a hole, and hid himself for some time; but the victor flew up to an eminent place, clapt his wings, and crowed out victory. An Eagle, who was watching for his prey near the place, saw him, and, making a swoop, trussed him up in his talons, and carried him off. The Cock that had been beaten, perceiving this, soon quitted his hole, and, shaking off all remembrance of his late disgrace, gallanted the hens with all the intrepidity imaginable.

### MORAL.

Before honour is humility. We must not be too much elevated by prosperity lest we meet a grievous fall.

THE FIGHTING COCK AND EAGLE.

## FABLE XI.

### THE DIAMOND AND THE LOADSTONE.

A DIAMOND, of great beauty and lustre, observing, not only many other gems of a lower class ranged together with himself in the same cabinet, but a Loadstone likewise placed not far from him, began to question the latter how he came there, and what pretensions he had to be ranked among the precious stones ; he, who appeared to be no better than a mere flint, a sorry, coarse, rusty-looking pebble, without any the least shining quality to advance him to such an honour ; and concluded with desiring him to keep his distance, and pay a proper respect to his superiors.

"I find," said the Loadstone, "you judge by external appearances, and condemn without due examination ; but I will not act so ungenerously by you. I am willing to allow you your due praise : you are a pretty bauble ; I am mightily delighted to see you glitter and sparkle ; I look upon you with pleasure and surprise ; but I must be convinced you are of some sort of use before I acknowledge that you have any real merit, or treat you with that respect which you seem to demand. With regard to myself, I confess my deficiency in outward beauty; but I may venture to say, that I make amends by my intrinsic qualities. The great improvement of navigation is entirely owing to me. By me the distant parts of the world have been made known and are accessible to each other; the remotest nations are connected together, and all, as it were, united into one common society; by a mutual intercourse they relieve one another's wants, and all enjoy the several blessings peculiar to each. The world is indebted to me for its wealth, its splendour, and its power; and the arts and sciences are, in a great measure, obliged to me for their improvements, and their continual increase. All these blessings I am the origin of; for by my aid it is that man is enable to construct that valuable instrument, the Mariner's Compass."

MORAL.

Let dazzling stones in splendour glare;
Utility's the gem for wear.

## FABLE XII.

### THE BEAR AND THE BEES.

A BEAR happened to be stung by a Bee; and the pain was so acute, that in the madness of revenge he ran into the garden, and overturned the hive. This outrage provoked their anger to such a degree that it brought the fury of the whole swarm upon him. They attacked him with such violence that his life was in danger, and it was with the utmost difficulty that he made his escape, wounded from head to tail. In this desperate condition, lamenting his misfortunes, and licking his sores, he could not forbear reflecting how much more advisable it had been to have patiently borne one injury, than by an unprofitable resentment to have provoked a thousand.

#### MORAL.

It is more prudent to acquiesce under an injury from a single person, then by an act of vengeance to bring upon us the resentment of a whole community.

## FABLE XIII.

### THE FROGS DESIRING A KING.

THE Frogs, living an easy, free life everywhere among the lakes and ponds, assembled together one day, in a very tumultuous manner, and petitioned Jupiter to let them have a king, who might inspect their morals, and make them live a little honester. Jupiter, being at that time in pretty good humour, was pleased to laugh heartily at their ridiculous request, and, throwing a little log down into the pool, cried, "There is a king for you!" The sudden splash which this made by its fall into the water, at first terrified them so exceedingly that they were afraid to come near it. But, in a little time, seeing it lie still without moving, they ventured, by degrees, to approach it; and at last, finding there was no danger, they leaped upon it, and, in short, treated it as familiarly as they pleased. But, not contented with so insipid a king as this was, they sent their deputies to petition again for another sort of one; for this they neither did nor could like. Upon that he sent them a Stork, who, without any ceremony, fell devouring and eating them up, one after another, as fast as he could. Then they applied themselves privately to Mercury, and got him to speak to Jupiter in their behalf, that he would be so good as to bless them again with another king, or restore them to their former state. "No," says he; "since it was their own choice, let the obstinate wretches suffer the punishment due to their folly."

### MORAL.

This fable teaches that it is better to be content with our present condition, however bad we may think it, than, by ambitious change, to risk making it worse.

—o—

## FABLE XIV.

### THE FOX AND THE BOAR.

THE Boar stood whetting his tusks against an old tree. The Fox, who happened to come by at the same time, asked him why he made those martial preparations of whetting his teeth, since there was no enemy near, that he could perceive. "That may be, Master Reynard," says the Boar, "but we should scour up our arms, while we have leisure, you know; for, in time of danger, we shall have something else to do."

### MORAL.

It is well to have preparations made for all emergencies, that when we are placed in any difficult position we may be calm and self-possessed. These preparations are best made in times of leisure.

c

## FABLE XV.

### THE VINE AND THE GOAT.

A GOAT having taken shelter from the heat of the sun under the broad leaves of a shady-spreading vine, began to crop and eat them ; by this means, the branches being put into a rustling motion, he drew the eyes of some hunters who were passing that way, and, seeing the vine stir, thought some wild beast had taken covert there; they shot their arrows at a venture, and killed the Goat, who, before he expired, uttered his dying words to this purpose : " Ah ! I suffer justly for my ingratitude, who could not forbear doing an injury to the vine that had so kindly afforded me shelter."

### MORAL.

Ingratitude is a great crime, and from which we should seek earnestly to be preserved. He that is capable of injuring his benefactor, what would he scruple to do towards another?

THE VINE AND THE GOAT.

## FABLE XVI.

### THE DISCONTENTED HORSE.

As JUPITER once was receiving petitions
From birds and from beasts of all ranks and conditions;
With an eye full of fire, and mane quite erect,
Which, I'm sorry to say, shewed but little respect,
The Horse went as near as he dared to the throne,
And thus made his donkey-like sentiments known:

"For beauty of symmetry, fleetness, and force,
It is said that all animals yield to the Horse;
While my spirit I feel, and my figure I view
In the brook, I'm inclined to believe it is true;
But still, mighty Jupiter, still, by your aid,
In my form might some further improvements be made.
To run is my duty, and swifter and stronger
I surely should go, were my legs to be longer:
And as man always places a seat on my back,
I should have been made with a saddle or sack;
It had saved *him* much trouble, on journies departing,
And *I* had been constantly ready for starting."

Great Jupiter smiled (for he laughed at the brute,
As he saw more of folly than vice in his suit),
And striking the earth with omnipotent force,
A Camel rose up near the terrified Horse :
He trembled—he started—his mane shook with fright,
And he staggered half round, as preparing for flight.

"Behold!" exclaimed Jove, "there an animal stands
With both your improvements at once to your hands:
His legs are much longer; the hump on his back
Well answers the purpose of saddle or sack:
Of your shapes, tell me, which is more finished and trim?
Speak out, silly Horse, would you wish to be him?"

The Horse looked abashed, and had nothing to say
And Jove, with reproaches, thus sent him away :
"Begone, till you gratefully feel and express
Your thanks for the blessings and gifts you possess.
The Camel, though plain, is mild, useful, and good;
You are handsome, but proud, discontented and rude."

## FABLE XVII.

### THE MOUNTAIN IN LABOUR.

A RUMOUR once prevailed that a neighbouring mountain was in labour; it was affirmed that she had been heard to utter prodigious groans; and a general expectation had been raised that some extraordinary birth was at hand.

Multitudes flocked in much eagerness to be witnesses of the wonderful event, one expecting her to be delivered of a giant, another of some enormous monster, and all were in earnest expectation of something grand and astonishing; when, after waiting with great impatience a considerable time, behold, out crept a MOUSE.

### MORAL.

To raise uncommon expectations renders an ordinary event ridiculous.

## FABLE XVIII.

### THE FOX AND THE STORK.

THE Fox, though in general more inclined to roguery than wit, had once a strong inclination to play the wag with his neighbour the Stork. He accordingly invited her to dinner in due form. But when she came to the table, the

Stork found it consisted entirely of different soups, served in broad, shallow dishes, so that she could only dip the end of her bill in them, but could not possibly satisfy her hunger. The Fox lapped them up very readily, and every now and then addressing himself to his guest, desired to know how she liked her entertainment, hoped that everything was to her liking, and protested he was very sorry to see her eat so sparingly.

The Stork, perceiving she was jested with, took no notice, but pretended to like every dish extremely; and, at parting, pressed the Fox so earnestly to return her visit that he could not, in civility, refuse.

The day arrived, and he repaired to his appointment. But, to his great dismay, he found the dinner was composed of minced meat, served up in long, narrow-necked bottles; so that he was only tantalized with the sight of what it was impossible for him to taste. The Stork thrust in her long bill, and helped herself very plentifully; then, turning to Reynard, who was eagerly licking the outside of a jar where some sauce had been spilled, "I am very glad," said she, smiling, "that you appear to have so good an appetite. I hope you will make as hearty a dinner at my table as I did the other day at yours." The Fox hung down his head, and looked very much displeased. "Nay, nay!" said the Stork; "don't pretend to be out of humour about the matter; they that cannot take a jest should never make one.

# FABLE XIX.

## THE HORSE AND THE STAG.

THE Stag, with his sharp horns, got the better of the Horse, and drove him clear out of the pasture where they used to feed together. So the latter craved the assistance of man, and, in order to receive the benefit of it, suffered him to put a bridle into his mouth, and a saddle upon his back. By this means he entirely defeated his enemy, but was mightily disappointed when, upon returning thanks, and desiring to be dismissed, he received this answer: "No; I never knew before how useful a drudge you were; now I have found out what you are good for, you may depend upon it, I will keep you to it."

### MORAL.

Help yourself, if you can do so; but at any rate, before you seek the assistance of a powerful man, be sure that the help he gives you will be disinterested, or you may find that in helping you he may put you under obligations fatal to liberty.

## FABLE XX.

### THE LION WOUNDED.

A MAN, who was very skilful with his bow, went up into the forest to hunt. At his approach, there was a great consternation and rout among the wild beasts, the Lion alone showing any determination to fight. "Stop," said the Archer to him, "and await my messenger, who has somewhat to say to you." With that, he sent an arrow after the Lion, and wounded him in the side. The Lion, smarting with anguish, fled into the depths of the forest; but a Fox, seeing him run, bade him take courage, and face his enemy. "No," said the Lion, "you will not persuade me to that; for if the messenger he sends is so sharp, what must be the power of him who sends it?"

### MORAL.

It is better to yield to a superior force than foolishly brave its power.

THE LION WOUNDED.

## FABLE XXI.

### THE ASS IN THE LION'S SKIN.

An Ass, finding a Lion's skin, disguised himself with it, and ranged about the forest, putting all the beasts that saw him into bodily fear. After he had diverted himself thus for some time, he met a Fox, and, being desirous to frighten him too, as well as the rest, he leapt at him with some fierce ness, and endeavoured to imitate the roaring of the Lion.

"Your humble servant," says the Fox, " if you had held your tongue, I might have taken you for a Lion, as others did; but now you bray I know who you are."

### MORAL.

A silent man may pass for a wise man, but when we hear him speak we are able to form an estimate of his value.

—o—

## FABLE XXII.

### JUPITER AND THE FARMER.

'Tis said, that Jove had once a farm to let,
　　And sent down Mercury, his common crier,
To make the most that he could get;
　　Or sell it to the highest buyer.

To view the premises the people flocked:
    And, as 'tis usual in such case,
    Began to run them down apace;
The soil was poor, the farm ill stocked:
    In short, a barren, miserable place,
    Scarce worth th' expense to draw a lease.

One bolder, tho' not wiser than the rest,
    Offered to pay in so much rent,
    Provided he had Jove's consent
To guide the weather just as he thought best;
    Or wet, or dry; or cold, or hot;
    Whate'er he asked should be his lot;

To all which Jove gave a consenting nod.
    The seasons now obsequious stand,
    Quick to obey their lord's command,
And now the Farmer undertakes the god;
    Now calls for sunshine, now for rains,
    Dispels the clouds, the wind restrains;

But still confined within his farm alone,
He makes a climate all his own;
    For when he sheds, or when he pours,
    Refreshing dews, or soaking showers,

His neighbours never share a drop;
So much the better for their crop;
Each glebe a plenteous harvest yields;
Whilst our director spoils his fields.

Next year, he tries a different way;
New moulds the seasons, and directs again;
But all in vain:
His neighbour's grounds still thrive while his decay.

What does he do in this sad plight?
For once he acted right:
He to the god his fate bemoaned,
Asked pardon, and his folly owned.
Jove, like a tender master, fond to save,
His weakness pityed, and his fault forgave.

MORAL.

He, who presumes the ways of heaven to scan,
Is not a wise, nor yet a happy man:
In this firm truth securely we may rest,—
Whatever Providence ordains is best;
Had man the power, he'd work his own undoing;
To grant his will would be to cause his ruin.

## FABLE XXIII.

### THE VAIN JACKDAW.

A CERTAIN Jackdaw was so proud and ambitious that, not contented to live within his own sphere, he picked up the feathers which fell from the Peacocks, stuck them among his own, and very confidently introduced himself into an assembly of those beautiful birds. They soon found him out, stripped him of his borrowed plumes, and falling upon him with their sharp bills, punished him as his presumption deserved.

Upon this, full of grief and affliction, he returned to his old companions, and would have flocked with them again ; but they, knowing his late life and conversation, industriously avoided him, and refused to admit him into their company; and one of them, at the same time, gave him this serious reproof: "If, friend, you could have been contented with your station, and had not disdained the rank in which nature had placed you, you had not been used so scurvily by those amongst whom you introduced yourself, nor suffered the notorious slight which we now think ourselves obliged to put upon you."

MORAL.

Great evils arise from vanity; for when we try to place ourselves in a position for which we are not fit, we are liable to be laughed at, and, when we would return to our former state, we find we have lost the esteem of our former friends.

———o———

## FABLE XXIV.

### THE VIPER AND THE FILE.

A VIPER, crawling into a smith's shop to seek for something to eat, cast her eyes upon a File, and darting upon it in a moment, "Now I have you," said she, "and so you may help yourself how you can; but you may take my word for it that I shall make a fine meal of you before I think of parting with you." "Silly wretch!" said the File, as gruff as could be, "you had much better be quiet, and let me alone; for, if you gnaw for ever, you will get nothing but your trouble for your pains. Make a meal of me, indeed! why, I myself can bite the hardest iron in the shop; and if you go on with your foolish nibbling I shall tear all the teeth out of your spiteful head before you know where you are."

MORAL.

Take care that you never strive with those who are too strong for you, nor do spiteful things, lest you suffer for it.

# FABLE XXV.

## THE WOLF AND THE LAMB.

ONE hot, sultry day, a Wolf and a Lamb happened to come just at the same time to quench their thirst in the stream of a clear, silver brook, that ran tumbling down the side of a rocky mountain. The Wolf stood upon the higher ground, and the Lamb at some distance from him down the current. However, the Wolf, having a mind to pick a quarrel with him, asked him what he meant by disturbing the water, and making it so muddy that he could not drink, and at the same time demanded satisfaction. The Lamb, frightened at this threatening charge, told him, in a tone as mild as possible, that, with humble submission, he could not conceive how that could be, since the water which he drank ran down from the Wolf to him, and therefore it could not be disturbed so far up the stream. "Be that as it will," replies the Wolf, "you are a rascal; and I have been told that you treated me with ill-language behind my back about half a year ago." "Upon my word," says the Lamb, "the time you mention was before I was born. The Wolf finding it to no purpose to argue any longer against truth, fell into a great passion, snarling and foaming at the mouth, as if he

THE WOLF AND THE LAMB.

had been mad ; and, drawing nearer to the Lamb, "Sirrah," said he, " if it was not you, it was your father, and that's all one." So he seized the poor innocent, helpless thing, tore it to pieces, and made a meal of it.

### MORAL.

Bad men, who wish to quarrel, will always find a pretence; if they can find no true grounds, they will resort to those which are false.

——o——

## FABLE XXVI.

### THE OLD BULLFINCH AND YOUNG BIRDS.

It chanced, that, on a winter's day,
But warm and bright, and calm as May,
The birds, conceiving a design
To forestall sweet St. Valentine,
In many an orchard, copse, and grove,
Assembled on affairs of love ;
And with much twitter and much chatter,
Began to agitate the matter.

At length, a Bullfinch, who could boast
More years and wisdom than the most,
Entreated, opening wide his beak,
A moment's liberty to speak ;
And, silence publicly enjoined,
Delivered briefly thus his mind :


" My friends, be cautious how ye treat
The subject upon which we meet ;
I fear we shall have winter yet."


A Finch, whose tongue knew no control,
With golden wing, and satin poll,
A last year's bird, who ne'er had tried
What marriage means, thus pert replied :


" Methinks, the gentleman," quoth she,
" Opposite, in the apple-tree,
By his good will, would keep us single,
'Till yonder heaven and earth shall mingle ;
Or (which is likelier to befall)
'Till death exterminate us all.
I marry without more ado ;
My dear Dick Redcap, what say you ?"

Dick heard; and tweedling, ogling, bridling,
Turning short round, strutting, and sidling,
Attested glad his approbation
Of an immediate conjugation.
Their sentiments so well express'd,
Influenced mightily the rest;
All pair'd, and each pair built a nest.

But though the birds were thus in haste,
The leaves came on not quite so fast;
And destiny, that sometimes bears
An aspect stern on man's affairs,
Not altogether smil'd on theirs.

The wind, that late breath'd gently forth,
Now shifted east, and east by north;
Bare trees and shrubs but ill, you know,
Could shelter them from rain or snow;
Stepping into their nests, they paddled,
Themselves were chill'd, their eggs were addled;
Soon every father bird, and mother,
Grew quarrelsome, and peck'd each other;
Parted without the least regret,
Except that they had ever met;
And learn'd in future to be wiser
Than to neglect a good adviser.

D

MORAL.

Young folks, who think themselves so wise,
That old folks' counsel they despise,
Will find, when they too late repent,
Their folly prove their punishment.

—o—

# FABLE XXVII.

### THE MOUSE AND THE WEASEL.

A LITTLE starveling rogue of a Mouse had, with much pushing application, made his way through a small hole in a corn-basket, where he stuffed and crammed so plentifully, that, when he would have retired the way he came, he found himself too plump, with all his endeavours, to accomplish it. A Weasel, who stood at some distance, and had been diverting himself with beholding the vain efforts of the little fat thing, called to him, and said, "Harkee, honest friend; if you have a mind to make your escape, there is but one way for it: contrive to grow as poor and lean as you were when you entered, and then, perhaps, you may get off."

MORAL.

If evil habits have got a man into difficulties, there is no surer way to extricate himself than, by God's help, to cast those habits off.

# FABLE XXVIII.

### THE OLD HOUND.

An old Hound, who had been an excellent good one in his time, and given his master great sport and satisfaction in many a chase, at last, by the effect of years, became feeble and unserviceable.

However, being in the field one day when the Stag was almost run down, he happened to be the first that came in with him, and seized him by one of his haunches; but his decayed and broken teeth not being able to keep their hold, the deer escaped and threw him quite out. Upon which his master, being in a great passion, and going to strike him, the honest old creature is said to have barked out this apology. "Ah! do not strike your poor old servant; it is not my heart and inclination, but my strength and speed that fail me. If what I now am displeases you, pray don't forget what I have been."

### MORAL.

Past services should never be forgotten.

## FABLE XXIX.

### THE CHARGER AND THE ASS

THE Horse, adorned with his great war-saddle, and champing his foaming bridle, came thundering along the way, and made the mountains echo with his loud, shrill neighing. He had not gone far before he overtook an Ass, who was labouring under a heavy burthen, and moving slowly on in the same track with himself. Immediately he called out to him, in a haughty, imperious tone, and threatened to trample him in the dirt, if he did not make way for him. The poor, patient Ass, not daring to dispute the matter, quietly got out of his way as fast as he could, and let him go by. Not long after this, the same Horse, in an engagement with the enemy, happened to be shot in the eye, which made him unfit for show or any military business; so he was stript of his fine ornaments, and sold to a carrier. The Ass, meeting him in this forlorn condition, thought that now it was his time to speak; and so, says he, "Heyday, friend, is it you? Well, I always believed that pride of yours would one day have a fall."

### MORAL.

Pride and haughtiness are foreign to really great men. Those who show it, when in their high estate, if the wheel of fortune should change, instead of friendship or pity, will meet with nothing but contempt.

THE CHARGER AND THE ASS.

## FABLE XXX.

### THE COLT AND THE FARMER.

A COLT, for blood and mettled speed,
The choicest of the running breed,
Of youthful strength and beauty vain,
Refused subjection to the rein.

In vain the groom's officious skill
Opposed his pride, and checked his will;
In vain the master's forming care
Restrained with threats, or soothed with prayer:
Of freedom proud, and scorning man,
Wild o'er the spacious plain he ran.

Where'er luxuriant Nature spread
Her flowery carpet o'er the mead,
Or bubbling streams soft gliding pass
To cool and freshen up the grass,
Disdaining bounds, he cropped the blade,
And wantoned in the spoil he made.

In plenty thus the summer passed;
Revolving winter came at last :
The trees no more a shelter yield ;
The verdure withers from the field :
Perpetual snows invest the ground ;
In icy chains the streams are bound :
Cold, nipping winds, and rattling hail,
His lank, unsheltered sides assail.

As round he cast his rueful eyes,
He saw the thatched-roof cottage rise :
The prospect touched his heart with cheer,
And promised kind deliverance near.
A stable, erst his scorn and hate,
Was now become his wished retreat ;
His passion cool, his pride forgot,
A Farmer's welcome yard he sought.

The master saw his woful plight,
His limbs, that tottered with his weight,
And, friendly, to the stable led,
And saw him littered, dressed, and fed.
In slothful ease all night he lay ;
The servants rose at break of day ;
The market calls.   Along the road
His back must bear the pond'rous load ;

In vain he struggles or complains,
Incessant blows reward his pains.
To-morrow varies but his toil :
Chained to the plough, he breaks the soil ;
While scanty meals at night repay
The painful labours of the day.

Subdued by toil, with anguish rent,
His self-upbraidings found a vent.
"Wretch that I am !" he sighing said,
" By arrogance and folly led ;
Had but my restive youth been brought
To learn the lesson nature taught,
Then had I, like my sires of yore,
The prize from every courser bore.
Now, lasting servitude's my lot,
My birth contemned, my speed forgot ;
Doomed am I, for my pride, to bear
A living death from year to year."

### MORAL.

He who disdains control, will only gain
A youth of pleasure for an age of pain.

## FABLE XXXI.

### THE LARK AND HER YOUNG ONES.

A LARK, who had young ones in a field of corn almost ripe, was under some fear lest the reapers should come to reap it before her young brood was fledged and able to remove from that place. She, therefore, upon flying abroad to look for food, left this charge with them—to take notice what they heard talked of in her absence, and tell her of it when she came back again.

When she was gone, they heard the owner of the corn call to his son: "Well," says he, "I think this corn is ripe enough. I would have you go early to-morrow, and desire our friends and neighbours to come and help us to reap it." When the old Lark came home, the young ones fell a quivering and chirping round her, and told her what had happened, begging her to remove them as fast as she could. The mother bid them be easy: "For," said she, "if the owner depends on his friends and neighbours, I am pretty sure the corn will not be reaped to-morrow."

Next day, she went out again, leaving the same orders as before. The owner came, and staid, expecting his friends; but the sun grew hot, and nothing was done, for not a soul came to help them. Then says he to his son, "I perceive these friends of ours are not to be depended upon; so you must go to your uncles and cousins, and tell them I desire they would be here betimes to-morrow morning, to help us to reap." Well, this the young ones, in a great fright, reported also to their mother. "If that be all," says she, "do not be frightened, dear children; for kindred and relations are not so very forward to serve one another; but take particular notice what you hear said next time, and be sure you let me know it."

She went abroad next day, as usual; and the owner, finding his relations as slack as the rest of his neighbours, said to his son, "Harkee, George; get a couple of good sickles ready against to-morrow morning, and we will even reap the corn ourselves." When the young ones told their mother this, "Then," said she, "we must be gone indeed; for, when a man undertakes to do his business himself, it is not so likely he will be disappointed." So she removed her young ones at once, and the corn was reaped next day by the good man and his son.

MORAL.

Never depend on the assistance of others. No business is so sure to be done as that which a man sets about doing himself.

## FABLE XXXII.

### THE FOX AND THE CROW.

A Crow, having taken a piece of cheese out of a cottage window, flew up with it into a high tree in order to eat it; which the Fox observing, came and sat underneath, and began to compliment the Crow upon the subject of her beauty. "I protest," says he, "I never observed it before, but your feathers are of a more delicate white than any that ever I saw in my life! Ah! what a fine shape and graceful turn of body is there! And I make no question but you have a tolerable voice. If it is but as fine as your complexion, I do not know a bird that can pretend to stand in competition with you." The Crow foolishly believed all that the Fox said was true; but, thinking the Fox a little dubious as to her vocal powers, and having a mind to set him right in that matter, opened her mouth, and, in the same instant, let the cheese drop out of her mouth. This being what the Fox wanted, he caught it up in a moment, and trotted away, laughing to himself at the easy credulity of the Crow.

### MORAL.

When anyone is flattered as possessing qualities he ought to feel conscious he does not possess, let him beware lest the flatterers wish either to deprive him of some solid good, or to make him appear ridiculous in the eyes of others.

THE FOX AND THE CROW

## FABLE XXXIII.

### THE PEACOCK'S COMPLAINT.

THE Peacock presented a memorial to Juno, importing how hardly he thought he was used, in not having so good a voice as the Nightingale; how that bird was agreeable to every ear that heard it, while he was laughed at for his ugly, screaming noise, if he did but open his mouth.

The goddess, concerned at the uneasiness of her favourite bird, answered him very kindly to this purpose:—"If the Nightingale is blest with a fine voice, you have the advantage in point of beauty and size." "Ah!" says he, "but what avails my silent, unmeaning beauty, when I am so far excelled in voice?"

The goddess dismissed him, bidding him consider that the properties of every creature were appointed by the decree of Fate; to him beauty, to the Eagle strength, to the Nightingale a voice of melody, to the Parrot the faculty of speech, and to the Dove innocence; that each of these was contented with his own peculiar quality; and, unless he wished to be miserable, he must also learn to be equally satisfied.

MORAL.

The man who to his lot 's resigned
True happiness is sure to find;
While envy ne'er can mend the ill,
But makes us feel it keener still.

———o———

## FABLE XXXIV.

### THE STAG IN THE OX-STALL.

A STAG, roused from his thick covert in the midst of the forest, and driven hard by the hounds, made towards a farm-house, and, seeing the door of an ox-stall open, entered therein, and hid himself under a heap of straw. One of the oxen, turning his head about, asked him what he meant by venturing himself in such a place, where he was sure to meet his doom. "Ah!" said the Stag, "if you will but be so good as to favour me with your concealment, I hope I shall do well enough; I intend to make off again the first opportunity."

Well, he stayed there till towards night; in came the ox-man with a bundle of fodder, and never saw him. In short, all the servants of the farm came and went, and not one of them suspected anything of the matter. Nay, the bailiff himself came, according to form, and looked in, but walked away, no wiser than the rest. Upon this the Stag, ready to jump out of his skin for joy, began to return thanks to the good-natured Oxen, protesting that they were the most obliging people he had ever met with in his life.

After he had done his compliments, one of them answered him, gravely, "Indeed, we desire nothing more than to have it in our power to contribute to your escape, but there is a certain person you little think of who has a hundred eyes; if he should happen to come, I would not give this straw for your life."

In the meanwhile, home comes the master himself from a neighbour's, where he had been invited to dinner; and, because he had observed the cattle not look well of late, he went up to the rack, and asked why they did not give them more fodder; then, casting his eyes downward, "Heydey!" says he, "why so sparing of your litter? pray scatter a little more here. And these cobwebs —— But I have spoken so often that, unless I do it myself ——" Thus, as he went on, prying into everything, he chanced to look where the Stag's horns lay sticking out of the straw; upon which he raised a hue and cry, called his people about him, killed the Stag, and made a prize of him.

#### MORAL.

For a work to be done thoroughly, it ought to be done by oneself; the eye of a master is keener than that of a servant.

## FABLE XXXV.

### THE WIND AND THE SUN.

A DISPUTE once arose betwixt the North Wind and the Sun about the superiority of their power; and they agreed to try their strength upon a traveller, which should be able to get off his cloak first.

The North Wind began, and blew a very cold blast, accompanied with a sharp, driving shower. But this, and whatever else he could do, instead of making the man quit his cloak, obliged him to gird it about his body as close as possible.

Next came the Sun, who, breaking out from the thick, watery cloud, drove away the cold vapours from the sky, and darted his warm, sultry beams upon the head of the poor weather-beaten traveller. The man, growing faint with the heat, and unable to endure it any longer, first throws off his heavy cloak, and then flies for protection to the shade of a neighbouring grove.

### MORAL.

Soft and gentle means will often accomplish what force and fury can never effect.

## FABLE XXXVI.

### THE TRAVELLERS AND THE BEAR.

Two men, being about to travel through a forest together, mutually promised to stand by each other in any danger they should meet on the way. They had not gone far when a Bear came rushing towards them out of a thicket; upon which, one, being a light, nimble fellow, got up into a tree. The other, falling flat upon his face, and holding his breath, lay still, while the Bear came up and smelled at him; but that creature, supposing him to be a dead carcass, went back to the wood without doing him the least harm. When all was over, the man who had climbed the tree came down to his companion, and, with a pleasant smile, asked what the Bear had said to him; "For," says he, "I took notice that he clapped his mouth very close to your ear." "Why," replied the other, " he charged me to take care, for the future, not to put any confidence in such cowardly rascals as you are."

### MORAL.

Nothing is more common than to hear people profess friendship when there is no occasion for it; but he is a true friend who is ready to assist us in the time of danger and difficulty. Choose, therefore, friends whom you can depend on for such a time, and greatly value them.

## FABLE XXXVII.

### THE DOG AND THE SHADOW.

A dog, crossing a small rivulet, with a piece of flesh in his mouth, which he had stolen from a butcher's shop, saw his own shadow represented in the clear mirror of the limpid stream; and, believing it to be another dog who was carrying another piece of flesh, he could not forbear catching at it, but was so far from getting anything by his greedy design, that he dropped the piece he had in his mouth, which immediately sank to the bottom, and was irrecoverably lost.

### MORAL.

It is the just punishment of greediness to lose the substance by grasping at the shadow; while the man who would take what does not belong to him deserves to lose what he has.

THE DOG AND THE SHADOW.

## FABLE XXXVIII.

### THE HERMIT AND THE BEAR.

ONCE on a time, a mountain Bear
Lived in a forest drear, with no Bears near him;
    Fat, fierce, and sulky.
Nor man nor other beast approached his lair;
His neighbours all despise, or hate, or fear him.
    'Tis good to talk—to hold one's tongue—
    Though either in excess be wrong:
    Our hermit bulky,
So shaggy, sullen, taciturn, and rude,
Bear as he was, grew sick of solitude.

At the same time, by chance, retired
Far from the world, a man advanced in age,
    But stout and healthy.
Not with devotion's flame his heart was fired;
Not prayer and fasting occupied the sage;
    Though on mankind he shut his door,
    No vows of poverty he swore:
    The wight was wealthy.
But by some treacherous friend, or fair, betrayed,
He lived with plants, and communed with his spade.

E

High priest of Flora you might call him ;
Nor less was he the favourite of Pomona.
  But one day, walking,
 He found it dull ; and should some ill befall him,
In his sweet paradise, he felt alone,—Ah !
 For neither rose, nor pink, nor vine,
 Except in such a lay as mine,
  Are given to talking.
His head old Time had now long years heaped many on ;
So he resolved to look for some companion.  .

 On this important expedition—
But fearing his researches would be vain—
  The sage departed :
 Revolving deeply his forlorn condition,
He slowly mused along a narrow lane ;
 When on a sudden—unawares—
 A nose met his :—it was the Bear's !
  With fright he started.
Fear is a common feeling : he that wise is,
Although his fright be great, his fear disguises.

 Prudence suggested—" Stand your ground ;
'Tis hard to tur.   and harder still to dash on."
  Prudence prevails.
 'Twixt kindred minds a sympathy is found
Which lights up oft at sight a tender passion,

Where sexes are of different kind;
And oft 't will ties of friendship bind
    Between two males :
These magic signs our hermits, at a glance, see:
Each found he strongly pleased the other's fancy.


Bruin at compliments was awkward,
But was not long his sentiments in telling—
    " Old man, I like you ! "
The man replied, " Fair sir, you need not walk hard,
In half an hour you'll reach my humble dwelling.
I've milk, and various sorts of fruit,
If any should your palate suit,
    Take what may strike you ;
On me it will confer the highest pleasure
To spread before you all my garden's treasure."


On jogged the human Hermit with the Bear,
Like smoking Germans, few words interlarding;
    Though little said,
Finding their tempers suited to a hair,
They grew firm friends before they reached the garden.
    Each took his task, their moods the same,
    One dug, the other hunted game,
        And often sped;

And Bruin, o'er his friend a strict watch keeping,
Chased off the flies that haunted him when sleeping.

One afternoon, as in the sun
The weary Hermit took his usual nap,
     And at his post
The faithful Bear his daily work begun,
Giving full many a brush and gentle slap,
  With a light whisp of herbs sweet-scented,
  And thus the teasing flies prevented,
       That buzzing host,
From fixing on his sleeping patron's visage,
Sunk in the deep repose so fit for his age.

One blue-bottle his care defied;
No place could please him but the old man's nose,
     Quite unabashed.
The Bear, provoked, no means would leave untried;
At last, a vigorous, certain mode, he chose:
  Extending wide his heavy paw,
  And thrusting hard each crooked claw,
       The fly was smashed:
But his poor patron's face, so roughly patted,
All streamed with blood, and smooth his nose was
     flatted.

The Bear sneaked off to humble distance,
Seeing the damage he had done his friend;
   Who raged with smart.
But calling in philosophy's assistance,
Anger, he thought, his wounds would never mend,
   So coolly said, " Farewell, friend Bruin!
Since you have laid my face in ruin,
   'Tis time to part."

### MORAL.

All those must such mishaps expect to share,
Who, for a friend, think fit to take a Bear.

—*o*—

## FABLE XXXIX.

### THE SHEPHERD'S BOY AND THE WOLF.

A CERTAIN Shepherd's Boy, who kept sheep upon a common, in sport and wantonness would often cry out, " The Wolf! the Wolf!" By this means, he several times drew the husbandmen in an adjoining field from their work; who, finding themselves deluded, resolved for the future to take no notice of his alarm. Soon after the Wolf came indeed. The boy cried out in earnest; but no heed being given to his cries, the sheep were devoured by the Wolf.

### MORAL.

The notorious liar, besides the sin of the thing, will not be believed when, by chance, he tells the truth.

# FABLE XL.

## THE FAWN AND HER MOTHER.

A HIND was one day stamping with her foot, and bellowing so loudly that the whole herd quaked for fear, when one of her little Fawns, coming up to her, said, "Mother, what is the reason that you, who are so strong and bold at all other times, if you do but hear the cry of the hounds, are so afraid of them?" "What you say is true," replied the Hind; "though I know not how to account for it. I am, indeed, vigorous and strong enough, and often resolve that nothing shall ever dismay my courage; but, alas! I no sooner hear the voice of a hound than all my spirits fail me, and I cannot help making off as fast as my legs can carry me."

### MORAL.

When we have done all, Nature will remain what she was. There is no arguing a coward into courage.

THE FAWN AND HER MOTHER.

# FABLE XLI.

### THE TORTOISE AND THE EAGLE.

THE Tortoise, weary of his condition, by which he was confined to creep upon the ground, and being ambitious to have a prospect, and look about him, gave out that, if any bird would take him up into the air, and show him the world, he would reward him with the discovery of many precious stones, which he knew were hidden in a certain part of the earth.

The Eagle undertook to do as he desired, and, when he had performed his commission, demanded the reward. But, finding the Tortoise could not make good his words, he stuck his talons into the softer parts of his body, and made him a sacrifice to his revenge.

### MORAL.

He that, to secure an advantage, deceives his friend by an untruth, will surely suffer for it when he is detected.

## FABLE XLII.

### THE BROTHER AND SISTER.

A CERTAIN Man had two children, a Son and a Daughter— the Boy handsome enough, the Girl not quite so comely. They were both very young, and happened one day to be playing near the looking-glass, which stood on their mother's toilet. The Boy, pleased with the novelty of the thing, viewed himself for some time, and in a wanton, roguish manner observed to the Girl how handsome he was. She resented the insult, and ran immediately to her father, and, with a great deal of aggravation, complained of her brother, particularly for having acted so effeminate a part as to look in a glass, and meddle with things which belong to women only. The father, embracing them both with much tender- ness and affection, told them that he should like to have them both look in the glass every day; "To the intent that you," says he to the Boy, "if you think that face of yours handsome, may not disgrace and spoil it by an ugly temper and a bad behaviour; and that you, " added he, addressing the Girl, "may make up for the defects of your person by the sweetness of your manners and the excellence of your understanding."

### MORAL.

A well-informed mind is better than a handsome person.

## FABLE XLIII.

### THE SHEPHERD'S DOG AND THE WOLF.

A WOLF, with hunger fierce and bold,
Ravaged the plains, and thinned the fold;
Deep in the wood secure he lay,
The thefts of night regaled the day.
In vain the shepherd's wakeful care
Had spread the toils, and watched the snare;
In vain the Dog pursued his pace,
The fleeter robber mocked the chase.

As Lightfoot ranged the forest round,
By chance his foe's retreat he found:
" Let us awhile the war suspend,
And reason as from friend to friend."
" A truce !" replies the Wolf.   'Tis done.
The Dog the parley thus begun :—

" How can that strong, intrepid mind
Attack a weak, defenceless kind?
Those jaws should prey on nobler food,
And drink the boar's and lion's blood;

Great souls with generous pity melt,
Which coward tyrants never felt.
How harmless is our fleecy care!
Be brave, and let thy mercy spare."

"Friend," says the Wolf, "the matter weigh:
Nature designed us beasts of prey;
As such, when hunger finds a treat,
'Tis necessary Wolves should eat.
If, mindful of the bleating weal,
Thy bosom burn with real zeal,
Hence, and thy tyrant lord beseech;
To him repeat the moving speech.
A Wolf eats sheep but now and then;
Ten thousands are devoured by men."

MORAL.

An open foe may prove a curse,
But a pretended friend is worse.

## FABLE XLIV.

### THE COVETOUS MAN.

A POOR covetous wretch, who had scraped together a good parcel of money, went and dug a hole in one of his fields and hid it. The great pleasure of his life was to go and look upon this treasure once a day at least; which one of his servants observing, and guessing there was something more than ordinary in the place, came at night, found it, and carried it off. The next day, returning as usual to the scene of his delight, and perceiving it had been stolen away from him, he tore his hair for grief, and uttered the doleful complaints of his despair to the woods and meadows. At last, a neighbour of his, who knew his temper, overhearing him, and being informed of the occasion of his sorrow, " Cheer up, man!" says he, "thou has lost nothing; there is the hole for thee to go and peep at still; and if thou canst but fancy thy money there, it will do just as well.

### MORAL.

Money, well used, has its full value; but when allowed to lie useless to others or to one's self, it possesses no more value than a heap of oyster shells. Avarice is, therefore, a silly as well as a sinful vice. Use your wealth in doing good, and its highest value will be attained.

## FABLE XLV.

### THE HARE AND THE TORTOISE.

A HARE twitted a Tortoise on account of his slowness, and vainly boasted of her own great speed in running. "Let us make a match," replied the Tortoise: "I'll run with you five miles for five pounds, and the Fox yonder shall be the umpire of the race." The Hare agreed, and away they both started together. But the Hare, by reason of her exceeding swiftness, outran the Tortoise to such a degree that she made a jest of the matter, and, finding herself a little tired, squatted in a tuft of fern that grew by the way, and took a nap, thinking that, if the Tortoise went by, she could at any time catch him up with all the ease imaginable. In the meanwhile the Tortoise came jogging on, with a slow but continued motion; and the Hare, out of a too great security and confidence of victory, oversleeping herself, the Tortoise arrived at the end of the race first.

### MORAL.

Industry and application will, in most cases, do more than quick and ready wit. The highest genius, without industry, will generally fail of any great exploit.

THE HARE AND THE TORTOISE.

## FABLE XLVI.

### THE HOG AND THE ACORNS.

One moonshiny night,
With a great appetite,
A Hog feasted on Acorns with all his might :
Quite pleased with his prize
Both in taste and in size,
While he ate he devoured the rest with his eyes.

You know, I'm in joke,
When I say that the oak,
Moved a *bough* to the grunter before she spoke ;
But you know, too, in fable,
We feel ourselves able
To make anything speak—tree, flower, or table.

Said the Oak, looking big,
" I think, Mr. Pig,
You might thank me for sending you fruit from my twig ;
But, you ill-behaved Hog !
You devour the prog,
And have no better manners, I think, than a dog."

He replied, looking up,
Though not ceasing to sup,
Till the Acorns were eaten—ay, every cup—
" I acknowledge, to you
My thanks would be due,
If from feelings of kindness my supper you threw.


" To-morrow, good dame,
Give my children the same,
And then you, with justice, may gratitude claim."


MORAL.

He merits no praise
To the end of his days,
Who to those who surround him no service conveys.


—o—

## FABLE  XLVII.

### THE COUNTRY MOUSE AND THE CITY MOUSE.

An honest, plain, sensible country Mouse is said to have
entertained at his hole one day a fine Mouse of the town.
Having formerly been playfellows together, they were old
acquaintances, which served as an apology for the visit.

However, as master of the house, he thought himself obliged to do the honours of it, in all respects, and to make as great a stranger of his guest as he possibly could. In order to this, he set before him a reserve of delicate grey pease and bacon, a dish of fine oatmeal, some parings of new cheese, and, to crown all with a dessert, a remnant of a charming mellow apple.

In good manners, he forebore to eat any of it himself, lest the stranger should not have enough; but, that he might seem to bear the other company, sat and nibbled a piece of wheaten straw very busily. At last, says the spark of the town, " Old croney, give me leave to be a little free with you. How can you bear to live in this nasty, dirty, melancholy hole here, with nothing but woods and meadows, mountains and rivulets about you? Do you not prefer the busy world to the chirping of birds, and the splendour of a court to the rude aspect of an uncultivated desert? Come, take my word for it, you will find it a change for the better. Stand not considering, but away this moment. Remember, we are not immortal, and therefore have no time to lose. Make sure of to-day, and spend it as agreeably as you can ; you know not what may happen to-morrow."

In short, these and such like arguments prevailed, and his country friend was resolved to go to town that night. So they both set out upon their journey, proposing to sneak

in after the close of the evening.  They did so, and about
midnight made their entry into a certain great house, where
there had been an extraordinary entertainment the day
before, and several tit-bits, which some of the servants had
purloined, were hid under a seat of a window.  The country
guest was immediately placed in the midst of a rich Persian
carpet; and now it was the courtier's turn to entertain, who,
indeed, acquitted himself in that capacity with the utmost
readiness and address, changing the courses as elegantly,
and tasting everything first as judiciously, as any clerk of the
kitchen.  The other sat and enjoyed himself like a delighted
epicure, tickled to the last degree with this new turn of his
affairs; when, on a sudden, a noise of somebody opening the
door made them start from their seats and scuttle in con-
fusion about the dining-room.  Our country friend, in particular, was ready to die with fear at the barking of a huge
Mastiff or two, which opened their throats just about the
same time, and made the whole house echo.

At last, recovering himself, "Well," says he, "if this be
your town life, much good may you do with it; give me my
poor, quiet hole again, with my homely but comfortable
grey pease."

MORAL.

Poverty and safety are preferable to luxury and danger.

## FABLE XLVIII.

### THE CAT AND THE MICE.

A CERTAIN house was much infested with Mice; but at last they got a Cat, who caught and ate every day some of them. The Mice, finding their numbers grow thin, consulted what was best to be done for the preservation of the public from the jaws of the devouring Cat. They debated and came to this resolution, that no one should go down below the upper shelf.

The Cat, observing the Mice no longer came down as usual, hungry and disappointed of her prey, had recourse to this stratagem :—She hung by her hind legs on a peg which stuck in the wall, and made as if she had been dead, hoping by this lure to entice the Mice to come down. She had not been in this posture long before a cunning old Mouse peeped over the edge of the shelf, and spoke thus :—"Ha! ha! my good friend, are you there? There you may be! I would not trust myself with you, though your skin were stuffed with straw."

### MORAL.

They that are wise will never trust those a second time who have deceived them once.

F

## FABLE XLIX.

### THE KID AND THE WOLF.

A KID, being mounted upon the roof of a lofty shed, and seeing a Wolf below, loaded him with all manner of reproaches. Upon which, the Wolf, looking up, replied, " Do not vaunt yourself, vain creature, and think you mortify me; for I look upon this ill language as not coming from you, but from the place that protects you."

### MORAL.

To rail or give bad language is wrong at all times; but when a man is protected by circumstances, it is cowardly, as well as wrong. The man who then uses it becomes a fit object of contempt to him that he reviles.

## FABLE L.

### THE COUNCIL OF HORSES.

Upon a time, a neighing Steed,
Who grazed among a numerous breed,
With mutiny had fired the train,
And spread dissension through the plain.

THE KID AND THE WOLF.

On matters that concerned the state
The council met in grand debate.
A Colt, whose eye-balls flamed with ire,
Elate with strength and youthful fire, .
In haste stepped forth before the rest,
And thus the listening throng addressed:—

" Good gods ! how abject is our race !
Condemned to slavery and disgrace !
Shall we our servitude retain,
Because our sires have borne the chain ?
Consider, friends, your strength and might;
'Tis conquest to assert your right.
How cumberous is the gilded coach !
The pride of man is our reproach.
Were we designed for daily toil,
To drag the ploughshare through the soil;
To sweat in harness through the road ;
To groan beneath the carrier's load ?
How feeble are the two-legged kind !
What force is in our nerves combined !
Shall, then, our nobler jaws submit
To foam and champ the galling bit ?
Shall haughty men my back bestride ?
Shall the sharp spur provoke my side ?

Forbid it, heavens! reject the rein,
Your shame, your infamy disdain.
Let him the Lion first control,
And still the Tiger's famished growl!
Let us, like them, our freedom claim;
And make him tremble at our name."

A general nod approved the cause,
And all the circle neighed applause;
When, lo! with grave and solemn pace,
A Steed advanced before the race,
With age and long experience wise;
Around he casts his thoughtful eyes,
And, to the murmurs of the train,
Thus spoke the Nestor of the plain :—

"When I had health and strength, like you,
The toils of servitude I knew.
Now, grateful man rewards my pains,
And gives me all these wide domains.
At will I crop the year's increase;
My latter life is rest and peace.
I grant, to man we lend our pains,
And aid him to correct the plains.
But doth not he divide the care,
Through all the labours of the year?

How many thousand structures rise,
To fence us from inclement skies!
For us he bears the sultry day,
And stores up all our winter's hay.
He sows, he reaps the harvest gain;
We share the toil, and share the grain."

The tumult ceased. The Colt submitted;
And, like his ancestors, was bitted.

MORAL.

Since every creature is decreed
To aid each other's mutual need;
Submit with a contented mind
To act the part by heaven assigned.

———o———

## FABLE LI.

### THE ASS AND THE LITTLE DOG.

THE Ass, observing how great a favourite a little Dog
was with his master, how much caressed, and fondled, and
fed with good bits at every meal, and for no other reason, as

he could perceive, but skipping and frisking about, wagging his tail, and leaping up in his master's lap, was resolved to imitate the same, and see whether such behaviour would not procure him the same favours. Accordingly, the master was no sooner come home from walking about his fields and gardens, and was seated in his easy chair, than the Ass, who observed him, came gamboling and braying towards him, in a very awkward manner. The master could not help laughing aloud at the odd sight. But the jest soon became earnest, when he felt the rough salute of the fore-feet, as the Ass, raising himself upon his hinder legs, pawed against his breast with a most loving air, and would fain have jumped into his lap. The good man, terrified at this outrageous conduct, and unable to endure the weight of so heavy a beast, cried out; upon which one of his servants, running in with a good stick, and laying heartily upon the bones of the poor Ass, soon convinced him that everyone who desires it is not qualified to be a favourite.

MORAL.

All men have not the same gifts of pleasing. It will be well, therefore, to keep in our own place; and, in that condition of life, to do our duty. By which we shall be most likely to give satisfaction.

## FABLE LII.

### THE LION AND THE FOUR BULLS.

FOUR Bulls, which had entered into a very strict friendship, kept always near one another, and fed together. The Lion often saw them, and as often wished to make one of them his prey; but though he could easily have subdued any of them singly, yet he was afraid to attack the whole when together, knowing they would have been too hard for him; and, there-fore, contented himself for the present with keeping at a distance. At last, perceiving no attempt was to be made upon them as long as their combination lasted, he took occa-sion, by whispers and hints, to foment jealousies and raise divisions among them.

This stratagem succeeded so well, that the Bulls grew cold and reserved towards one another, which soon after ripened into a downright hatred and aversion, and, at last, ended in a total separation. The Lion had now obtained his ends; and, as impossible as it was for him to hurt them while they were united, he found no difficulty, now they were parted, to seize and devour every Bull of them, one after another.

### MORAL.

Union is strength. Jealousy and envy, especially when fomented by whisperers, will destroy gradually the ties that make us safe against enemies.

# FABLE LIII.

## THE LEOPARD AND THE FOX.

THE Leopard one day took it into his head to value himself upon the great variety and beauty of his spots; and, truly, he saw no reason why even the lion should take place of him, since he could not show so beautiful a skin. As for the rest of the wild beasts of the forests, he treated them all, without distinction, in the most haughty and disdainful manner. But the Fox, being among them, went up to him with a great deal of spirit and resolution, and told him that he was mistaken in the value he was pleased to set upon himself, since people of judgment were not used to form their opinion of merit from an outside appearance, but by considering the good qualities and endowments with which the mind was stored within.

### MORAL.

Haughty beauty is an ungraceful thing. True beauty is always found in a setting of modesty, and then only appears the bright jewel that it is.

THE LEOPARD AND THE FOX.

## FABLE LIV.

### THE WARRIOR WOLF.

A young Wolf said aloud
To the listening crowd,
"I may well of my father's great courage be proud;
Wherever he came,
Flock, shepherd, or dame,
All trembled and fled at the sound of his name.
Did anyone spy
My papa coming by—
Two hundred or more—Oh! he made them all fly!
One day, by a blow,
He was conquered, I know;
But no wonder at last he should yield to a foe:
He yielded, poor fellow!
The conquering bellow
Resounds in my ears as my poor father's knell—Oh!"
A Fox then replied,
While, leering aside,
He laughed at his folly and vapouring pride:
"My chattering youth,
Your nonsense, forsooth,
Is more like a funeral sermon than truth.

Let history tell
How your old father fell;
And see if the narrative sounds as well.
Your folly surpasses,
Of monkeys all classes;
The beasts which he frightened, or conquered, were asses,
Except a few sheep,
When the shepherd, asleep,
The dog by his side for safety did keep.
Your father fell back,
Knocked down by a whack
From the very first bull that he dared to attack.
Away he'd have scoured,
But soon overpowered,
He lived like a thief, and he died like a coward."

—o—

## FABLE LV.

### THE BELLY AND THE MEMBERS.

In former days, when the Belly and the other parts of the body enjoyed the faculty of speech, and had separate views and designs of their own; each part, it seems, in particular, for himself, and in the name of the whole, took exception at the conduct of the Belly, and were resolved to grant him supplies no longer.

They said they thought it very hard that he should lead an idle, good-for-nothing life, spending and squandering away upon his own vile appetites all the fruits of their labour; and that, in short, they were resolved for the future to strike off his allowance, and let him shift for himself as well as he could.

The hands protested they would not lift a finger to keep him from starving; and the mouth wished he might never speak again if he took in the least bit of nourishment for him as long as he lived; and the teeth said, " May we be rotten if ever we chew a morsel for him for the future!" This solemn league and covenant was kept so long, until each of the rebel members pined away to the skin and bone, and could hold out no longer. Then they found there was no doing without the Belly, and that, as idle and insignificant as he seemed, he contributed as much to the maintenance and welfare of all the other parts as they did to his.

### MORAL.

Men are dependent upon their fellow-creatures, and it is foolish to expect we can do without the help of others.

# FABLE LVI.

### THE CUR, THE HORSE, AND THE SHEPHERD'S DOG.

A VILLAGE Cur, of snappish race,
The pertest puppy in the place,
Imagined that his treble throat
Was blessed with music's sweetest note;
In the mid road he basking lay,
The yelping nuisance of the way;
For not a creature passed along,
But had a sample of his song.

Soon as the trotting steed he hears,
He starts, he cocks his dapper ears;
Away he scours, assaults his hoof;
Now near him snarls, now barks aloof;
With shrill impertinence attends;
Nor leaves him till the village ends.

It chanced, upon his evil day,
A Pad came pacing down the way;

The Cur, with never-ceasing tongue,
Upon the passing traveller sprung.
The Horse, from scorn provoked to ire,
Flung backward; rolling in the mire,
The Puppy howled, and bleeding lay;
The Pad in peace pursued his way.

A Shepherd's Dog, who saw the deed,
Detesting the vexatious breed,
Bespoke him thus: " When coxcombs prate,
They kindle wrath, contempt, or hate;
Thy teasing tongue, had judgment tied,
Thou hadst not like a Puppy died."

MORAL.

Too late the forward youth will find
That jokes are sometimes paid in kind;
Or, if they canker in the breast,
He makes a foe who makes a jest.

## FABLE LVII.

### THE JACKDAW AND THE EAGLE.

An Eagle flew down from the top of a high rock, and settled upon the back of a lamb, and then, instantly flying up into the air again, bore his bleating prize aloft in his talons, A Jackdaw, who sat upon an elm, and beheld his exploit. resolved to imitate it.   So, flying upon the back of a ram, and entangling his claws in the wool, he fell a-chattering and attempting to fly; by which means he drew the observation of the shepherd upon him, who, finding his feet hampered in the fleece of the ram, easily took him, and gave him to his boys for their sport and diversion, saying, "The silly bird thought he was an Eagle; but, no doubt, by this time he has found out he is but a Jackdaw."

### MORAL.

A false estimate of our own abilities ever exposes us to ridicule, and often to danger.

THE JACKDAW AND THE EAGLE.

# FABLE LVIII.

## THE ASS AND THE LION HUNTING.

THE Lion took a fancy to hunt in company with the Ass; and, to make him the more useful, gave him instructions to hide himself in a thicket, and then to bray in the most .frightful manner that he could possibly contrive. "By, this means," says he, "you will rouse all the beasts within hearing of you, while I stand at the outlets and take them as they are making off." This was done; and the stratagem took effect accordingly. The Ass brayed most hideously, and the timorous beasts, not knowing what to make of it, began to scour off as fast as they could; when the Lion, who was posted at a convenient place, seized and devoured them as he pleased.

Having got his belly full, he called out to the Ass, and bid .him leave off braying, as he had had enough. Upon this the lop-eared brute came out of his ambush, and, approaching the Lion, asked him, with an air of conceit, "how he liked his performance." "Prodigiously," says he; "you did it so well, that I protest, had I not known your nature and temper, I might have been frightened myself."

## MORAL.

Boastful cowards may impose upon those who do not know them, but are held to be only ridiculous by those who do. Pompous persons who would wish themselves thought perfect Lions, when known are mostly found arrant Asses.

———

## FABLE LIX.

### THE WOLF IN SHEEP'S CLOTHING.

A WOLF clothing himself in the skin of a Sheep, and getting in among the flock, by this means took the opportunity to devour many of them. At last, the Shepherd discovered him, and cunningly fastened a rope about his neck, tying him up to a tree which stood hard by.

Some other Shepherds happening to pass that way, and observing what he was about, drew near, and expressed their wonder at it. "What," says one of them, "Brother, do you hang Sheep?" "No," replies the other; "I hang a Wolf whenever I catch him, though in the habit and garb of Sheep." Then he showed them their mistake, and they applauded the justice of the execution.

## MORAL.

Those who try to seem what they are not will not always thereby escape the punishment of what they are.

## FABLE LX.

### THE TWO BEES.

On a fine morning in May, two Bees set forward in quest of honey; the one, wise and temperate; the other, careless and extravagant. They soon arrived at a garden enriched with aromatic herbs, the most fragrant flowers, and the most delicious fruits. They regaled themselves for a time on the various dainties that were set before them: the one loading his thigh at intervals with provisions for the hive against the distant winter, the other revelling in sweets, without regard to anything but his present gratification.

At length, they found a wide-mouthed vial, that hung beneath the bough of a peach-tree, filled with honey ready tempered, and exposed to their taste in the most alluring manner. The thoughtless Epicure, spite of all his friend's remonstrances, plunged headlong into the vessel, resolving to indulge himself in all the pleasures of sensuality. The Philosopher, on the other hand, sipped a little with caution, but, being suspicious of danger, flew off to fruits and flowers; where, by the moderation of his meals, he improved his relish for the true enjoyment of them.

G

In the evening, however, he called upon his friend, to inquire whether he would return to the hive, but found him surfeited in sweets, which he was as unable to leave as to enjoy. Clogged in his wings, enfeebled in his feet, and his whole frame totally enervated, he was but just able to bid his friend adieu, and to lament, with his latest breath, that though a taste of pleasure may quicken the relish of life, an unrestrained indulgence is inevitable destruction.

MORAL.

Moderation rewards and intemperance punishes itself.

———◇———

## FABLE LXI.

### THE TURKEY AND THE ANT.

A Turkey, tired of common food,
Forsook the barn, and sought the wood;
Behind her ran her infant train,
Collecting here and there a grain.
"Draw near, my birds," the mother cries,
"This hill delicious fare supplies;
Behold the busy negro race,
See millions blacken all the place.

Fear not: like me, with freedom eat;
An Ant is most delightful meat.
How blessed, how envied were our life,
Could we but 'scape the poulterer's knife!
But man, cursed man, on Turkeys preys,
And Christmas shortens all our days.
Sometimes with oysters we combine;
Sometimes assist the savoury chine:
From the low peasant to the lord,
The Turkey smokes on every board;
Sure, men for gluttony are cursed,
Of the seven deadly sins, the worst."

An Ant, who climbed beyond her reach,
Thus answered from the neighbouring beech:
" Ere you remark another's sin,
Bid thy own conscience look within;
Control thy more voracious bill,
Nor, for a breakfast, nations kill."

### MORAL.

In other folks we faults can spy,
And blame the mote that dims their eye;
Each little speck and blemish find:
To our own stronger errors blind.

:

## FABLE LXII.

### THE DOG AND THE WOLF.

A LEAN, hungry, half-starved Wolf happened, one moon-shiny night, to meet a jolly, plump, well-fed Mastiff; and after the first compliments were passed, says the Wolf, "You look extremely well; I protest, I think I never saw a more graceful, comely person; but how comes it about, I beseech you, that you should live so much better than I? I may say, without vanity, that I venture fifty times more than you do, and yet I am almost ready to perish with hunger." The Dog answered very bluntly, "Why, you may live as well, if you do the same for it as I do." "Indeed! what is that?" says he. "Why," says the Dog, "only to guard the house at night, and keep it from thieves." "With all my heart," replies the Wolf, "for at present I have but a sorry time of it; and I think to change my hard lodging in the woods, where I endure rain, frost, and snow, for a warm roof over my head and enough of good victuals, will be no bad bargain." "True," says the Dog; "therefore you have nothing to do but to follow me."

Now, as they were jogging on together, the Wolf spied a

THE HOUSE DOG AND THE WOLF.

crease in the Dog's neck, and having a strange curiosity, could not forbear asking him what it meant! "Pugh! nothing," says the Dog. " Nay, but pray," says the Wolf. " Why," says the Dog, " if you must know, I am tied up in the day-time, because I am a little fierce, for fear I should bite people, and am only let loose at nights. But this is done with a design to make me sleep by day, more than anything else, and that I may watch the better in the night time; for, as soon as ever the twilight appears, out I am turned, and may go where I please. Then my master brings me plates of bones from the table with his own hands; and whatever scraps are left by any of the family, all fall to my share; for, you must know, I am a favourite with everybody. So you see how you are to live.—Come, come along; what is the matter with you?" "No," replied the Wolf, "I beg your pardon; keep your happiness all to yourself. Liberty is the word with me; and I would not be a king upon the terms you mention."

### MORAL.

The lowest condition of life, with freedom, is happier than the greatest without it. The bird of the air, though he roosts on a bough, has more real joy than the well-fed captive in a gilded cage.

## FABLE LXIII.

### THE SATYR AND THE TRAVELLER.

A SATYR, as he was ranging the forest in an exceedingly cold, snowy season, met with a Traveller half starved with the extremity of the weather. He took compassion on him, and kindly invited him home to a warm, comfortable cave he had in a hollow of a rock. As soon as they had entered and sat down, notwithstanding there was a good fire in the place, the chilled Traveller could not forbear blowing his finger-ends.

Upon the Satyr asking him why he did so, he answered that he did it to warm his hands. The honest Sylvan having seen little of the world, admired a man who was master of so valuable a quality as that of blowing heat; and, therefore, was resolved to entertain him in the best manner he could. He spread the table before him with dried fruits of several sorts, and produced a remnant of cold cordial wine, which, as the rigour of the season made very proper, he mulled with some warm spices, over the fire, and presented to his shivering guest. But this the Traveller thought fit to blow likewise; and upon the Satyr's demanding the reason why he blowed again, he replied, to cool the dish.

This second answer provoked the Satyr's indignation, as much as the first had kindled his surprise; so, taking the man by the shoulder, he thrust him out, saying he would have nothing to do with a wretch who had so vile a quality as to blow hot and cold with the same mouth.

MORAL.

Double dealing is always detestable. The man that blows hot and cold at the same time is not worthy to be trusted; the sooner we part from him the better.

----

## FABLE LXIV.

### THE BARLEY-MOW AND THE DUNGHILL.

As 'cross his yard, at early day,
A careful farmer took his way,
He stopped, and leaning on his fork,
Observed the flail's incessant work.
In thought he measured all his store;
His geese, his hogs, he numbered o'er;
In fancy weighed the fleeces shorn,
And multiplied the next year's corn.

A Barley-Mow, which stood beside,
Thus to its musing master cried:

"Say, good sir, is it fit or right,
To treat me with neglect and slight?
Me, who contribute to your cheer,
And raise your mirth with ale and beer!
Why thus insulted, thus disgraced,
And that vile Dunghill near me placed?
Are those poor sweepings of a groom,
That filthy sight, that nauseous fume,
Meet objects here?   Command it hence:
A thing so mean must give offence."

The humble Dunghill thus replied:
" Thy master hears, and mocks thy pride.
Insult not thus the meek and low;
In me thy benefactor know:
My warm assistance gave thee birth,
Or thou hadst perished low in earth:
But upstarts, to support their station,
Cancel at once all obligation."

## FABLE LXV.

### THE SHEEP-BITER AND SHEPHERD.

A CERTAIN Shepherd had a Dog, upon whose fidelity he relied very much; for whenever he had occasion to be absent himself, he committed the care and tuition of the flock to the charge of his Dog; and, to encourage him to do his duty cheerfully, he fed him constantly with sweet curds and whey, and sometimes threw him a crust or two. Yet, notwithstanding this, no sooner was his back turned, but the treacherous cur fell foul of the flock, and devoured the sheep, instead of guarding and defending them. The Shepherd being informed of this, was resolved to hang him; and the Dog, when the rope was about his neck, and he was just going to be hung, began to expostulate with his master, asking him, why he was so unmercifully bent against him, who was his own servant and creature, and had only committed two or three crimes, and why he did not rather execute vengeance upon the Wolf, who was a constant and declared enemy? "Nay," replies the Shepherd, "it is for that very reason that I think you ten times more deserving of death than he. From him I expected nothing but hostilities; and therefore could guard against him. You I depended upon as a just and faithful servant, and fed and encouraged you accordingly; and therefore your treachery is the more notorious, and your ingratitude the more unpardonable."

### MORAL.

A known enemy is better than a treacherous friend.

## FABLE LXVI.

### THE STAG AT THE POOL.

A STAG that had been drinking at a clear spring, saw himself in the water; and, pleased with the sight, stood long contemplating and surveying his shape and features from head to foot. "Ah!" says he, "what a glorious pair of branching horns are there! How gracefully do those antlers hang over my forehead, and give an agreeable turn to my whole face! If some other parts of my body were but in proportion to them, I would turn my back to nobody; but I have a set of such legs as really make me ashamed to see them. People may talk what they please of their conveniences, and what great need we stand in of them, upon several occasions; but, for my part, I find them so very slender and unsightly that I had as lief have none at all."

While he was giving himself these airs, he was alarmed with the noise of some huntsmen and a pack of hounds that had been just laid on upon the scent, and were making towards him.

Away he flees in some consternation, and, bounding nimbly over the plain, threw dogs and men at a vast distance behind him. After which, taking a very thick copse, he had the ill-fortune to be entangled by his horns in a thicket,

THE STAG AT THE POOL.

where he was held fast, till the hounds came in and pulled him down. Finding now how it was likely to go with him, in the pangs of death, he is said to have uttered these words:— "Unhappy creature that I am! I am too late convinced that what I prided myself in has been the cause of my undoing, and what I so much disliked was the only thing that could have saved me."

MORAL.

Beauty often becomes a snare and ruin, while solid virtue, though unadorned, gains respect. The latter, too, will mature with age, while the former will surely fade.

## FABLE LXVII.

### THE OLD SWALLOWS AND THE YOUNG BIRDS.

A SWALLOW, observing a husbandman employed in sowing hemp, called the little Birds together, and informed them what the farmer was about. He told them that hemp was the material from which the nets, so fatal to the feathered race, were composed; and advised them unanimously to join in picking it up, in order to prevent the consequences.

The Birds, either disbelieving his information, or neglecting his advice, gave themselves no trouble about the matter. In a little time, the hemp appeared above the ground. The friendly Swallow again addressed himself to them—told them it was not yet too late, provided they would immediately set about the work, before the seeds had taken too deep root. But, they still rejecting his advice, he forsook their society; repaired, for safety, to towns and cities; there built his habitation, and kept his residence.

One day, as he was skimming along the streets, he happened to see a great number of these very Birds, imprisoned in a cage, on the shoulders of a bird-catcher. "Unhappy wretches!" said he, "you now feel the punishment of your former neglect. But those who, having no foresight of their own, despise the wholesome admonition of their friends, deserve the mischiefs which their own obstinacy or negligence bring upon their heads."

MORAL.

This Fable teaches thoughtless youth
A most important moral truth :—
The seeds, which proved the young birds' ruin,
Are emblems of their own undoing,
Should they neglect, while yet 'tis time,
To pluck the early shoots of crime;
Or, in their own opinions wise,
The counsel of their friends despise.
For evil habits, left to grow,
Are ever sure to lead to woe;
But checked in time with vigorous hand,
Will bend to virtue's firm command.

## FABLE LXVIII.

### THE WAGGONER AND THE BUTTERFLY.

THE rain so soft had made the road,
That, in a rut, a waggon-load,
The poor man's harvest, (bitter luck!)
Sank down a foot, and there it stuck.
He whipped his horses, but in vain;
They pulled and splashed, and pulled again,
But vainly still; the slippery soil
Defied their strength, and mocked their toil.
Panting they stood, with legs outspread;
The driver stood, and scratched his head:
(A common custom, by-the-bye,
When people know not what to try,
Though not, it seems, a remedy).

A Butterfly, in flower concealed,
Had travelled with them from the field;
Who in the waggon was thrown up,
While feasting on a buttercup.

The panting of each labouring beast
Disturbed her at her fragrant feast;
The sudden stop, the driver's sigh,
Awoke her generous sympathy.
And, seeing the distressing case
She cried, while springing from her place,
(Imagining her tiny freight
A vast addition to the weight,)
"I must have pity—and be gone,
Now, master Waggoner, drive on."

### MORAL.

Do not admire this Butterfly,
Young reader; I will tell you why.
At first, goodnature seems a cause,
Why she should merit your applause;
But 'twas conceit that filled her breast:
Her self-importance made a jest
Of what might otherwise have claimed
Your praise,—but now she must be blamed.
Should any case occur, when you
May have some friendly act to do;
Give all *your feeble aid*—as such,
But estimate it not too much.

# FABLE LXIX.

### THE LION, THE BEAR, AND THE FOX.

A LION and a Bear quarrelling over the carcase of a Fawn, which they found in the forest, their title to him had to be decided by force of arms. The battle was severe and tough on both sides, and they fought it out, tearing and worrying one another so long, that, what with wounds and fatigue, they were so faint and weary, that they were not able to strike another stroke. Thus, while they lay upon the ground, panting and lolling out their tongues, a Fox chanced to pass by that way, who, perceiving how the case stood, very impudently stepped in between them, seized the booty which they had all this while been contending for, and carried it off. The two combatants, who lay and beheld all this, without having strength to stir and prevent it, were only wise enough to make this reflection :—" Behold the fruits of our strife and contention ! That villain, the Fox, bears away the prize, and we ourselves have deprived each other of the power to recover it from him."

### MORAL.

When fools quarrel, knaves get the prize of contention.

# FABLE LXX.

## THE FOX AND THE GRAPES.

In days of yore, when a young Fox would take more pains to get a bunch of grapes than a plump, fat goose, an arch young thief cast his eyes on a fine bunch which hung on the top of a poor man's vine, and made him lick his lips like a hound at the sight of a joint of meat. "Oh," said he, "how nice they look! I must have a taste of them, if I die for it;" and with that, up he jumped with all his might, but had the ill-luck not to reach the grapes; yet, as he could not find in his heart to leave them, he tried for them as long as he was able; so he leaped and jumped, and jumped and leaped, till at last he was glad to rest. But when he found all his pains were in vain, "Hang them!" said he, "I am sure they are not fit to eat, for they are as sour as crabs, and would set my teeth on edge for a whole week; and so I shall leave them for the next fool who may chance to come this way."

### MORAL.

Some men make light of that which is out of their reach, though at the same time in their hearts they know not what to do for want of it.

THE FOX AND THE GRAPES.

## FABLE LXXI.

### THE HARE AND MANY FRIENDS.

A HARE, who, in a civil way,
Complied with everything, like Gay,
Was known by all the bestial train,
Who haunt the wood, or graze the plain.

As forth she went, at early dawn,
To taste the dew-besprinkled lawn,
Behind she hears the hunter's cries,
And from the deep-mouthed thunder flies.
She starts, she stops, she pants for breath;
She hears the near approach of death;
She doubles, to mislead the hound,
And measures back her mazy round;
Till, fainting in the public way,
Half dead with fear, she gasping lay :—
What transport in her bosom grew,
When first the Horse appeared in view!

"Let me," says she, "your back ascend,
And owe my safety to a friend;

H

You know my feet betray my flight;
To friendship, ev'ry burthen's light."

The Horse replied,—"Poor, honest Puss!
It grieves my heart to see thee thus:
Be comforted,—relief is near;
For all our friends are in the rear."

She next the stately Bull implored,
And thus replied the mighty lord:—
"Since every beast alive can tell,
That I sincerely wish you well,
I may, without offence, pretend
To take the freedom of a friend.
Love calls me hence; a favourite cow
Expects me near yon barley-mow;
And when a lady's in the case,
You know, all other things give place.
To leave you thus may seem unkind;
But see,—the Goat is just behind."

The Goat remarked her pulse was high;
Her languid head, her heavy eye;
"My back," says she, "may do you harm;
The Sheep's at hand, and wool is warm."

The Sheep was feeble, and complained,
His sides a load of wool sustained;
Said he was slow; confessed his fears;
For Hounds eat Sheep as well as Hares.

She now the trotting Calf addressed,
To save from death a friend distressed.
"Shall I," says he, " of tender age,
In this important care engage?
Older and abler pass you by;
How strong are those! how weak am I!
Should I presume to bear you hence,
Those friends of mine may take offence.
Excuse me, then,—you know my heart;
But dearest friends, alas! must part.
How shall we all lament!—Adieu!
For see, the Hounds are just in view."

### MORAL.

Friendships are single: who depend
On many rarely find a friend.

# FABLE LXXII.

### THE COCK AND THE FOX.

A Cock, being perched among the branches of a lofty tree, crowed aloud, so that the shrillness of his voice echoed through the wood and invited a Fox to the place, who was prowling in that neighbourhood in quest of his prey. But Reynard, finding the Cock was inaccessible by reason of the height of his situation, had recourse to stratagem in order to decoy him down. So, approaching the tree, "Cousin," says he, "I am heartily glad to see you; but at the same time I cannot forbear expressing my uneasiness at the inconvenience of the place, which will not let me pay my respects to you in a handsomer manner; though I suppose you will come down presently, and thus the difficulty will be easily removed."

"Indeed, cousin," says the Cock, "to tell you the truth, I do not think it safe to venture upon the ground; for though I am convinced how much you are my friend, yet I may have the misfortune to fall into the clutches of some other beasts, and what will become of me then?" "Oh, dear!" says Reynard, "is it possible that you can be so ignorant, as not to know of the peace which has been lately proclaimed between all kinds of birds and beasts; and that we are for the future to forbear hostilities on all sides, and to live in the utmost love and harmony, and this, under the penalty of suffering the severest punishment that can be inflicted?" All this while the Cock seemed to give little attention to what was said, but stretched out his neck, as if he saw something at a distance.

"Cousin," says the Fox, "what is it that you look at so earnestly?" "Why," says the Cock, "I think I see a pack of hounds yonder, a little way off." "Oh, then," says the Fox, "your humble servant, I must begone." "Nay, pray cousin, do not go," says the Cock, "I am just coming down; surely you are not afraid of Dogs in these peaceable times?" "No, no," says he, "but ten to one whether they have heard of the proclamation yet."

### MORAL.

When rogues are met in their own strain, they are generally worsted. It is interesting to see the snares of the wicked defeated by the discreet management of the innocent. "Answer a fool according to his folly," is an old maxim.

## FABLE LXXIII.

### THE LION AND THE MOUSE.

A Lion, faint with heat and weary with hunting, was lying down to take his repose under the spreading boughs of a thick shady oak. It happened that while he slept, a company of scrambling mice ran over his back, and waked him; upon which, starting up, he clapped his paw upon one of them, and was just going to put it to death, when the little supplicant implored his mercy in a very moving manner, begging him not to stain his noble character with the blood of so despicable and small a beast.

The Lion, considering the matter, thought proper to do as he was desired, and immediately released his little trembling prisoner.

Not long after, while traversing the forest in pursuit of his prey, he chanced to run into the toils of the hunters, from whence, not being able to disengage himself, he set up a most hideous and loud roar.

The Mouse, hearing a voice, and knowing it to be the Lion's, immediately repaired to the place, and bid him fear nothing, for that he was his friend. Then straight he fell to work, and with his sharp little teeth gnawing asunder the knots and fastenings of the toils, set the royal brute at liberty.

### MORAL.

There is none so little, but that even the greatest may at some time or other stand in need of his assistance.

——*o*——

## FABLE LXXIV.

### THE TRUMPETER TAKEN PRISONER.

A Trumpeter, being taken prisoner in a battle, begged hard for quarter, declaring his innocence, and protesting that he neither had nor could kill any man, bearing no arms but only a trumpet, which he was obliged to sound at the word of command. "For that reason," replied his enemies, "we are determined not to spare you; for though you yourself never fight, yet with that wicked instrument of yours, you blow up animosity between other people, and so become the occasion of much bloodshed."

### MORAL.

The hand may rest quiet by the side, and yet the tongue be the means of doing more injury than a thousand hands.

## FABLE LXXV.

### THE MOUSE AND THE ELEPHANT.

A PERT young Mouse, but just arrived
From Athens, where some time he'd lived;
And daily to the portico,
To pick up learning, used to go;
Vain of the wisdom he had stored,
And of the books he had devoured;
Puffed up with pride and self-conceit,
. And proud to show his little wit,
Thus to an Elephant, one day,
He took it in his head to say:—

"Nay, not so pompous in your gait,
Because Dame Nature made you great;
I tell you, sir, your mighty size
Is of no value in my eyes;—
Your magnitude, I have a notion,
Is quite unfit for locomotion;
When journeying far, you often prove
How sluggishly your feet can move.

Now, look at me: I'm made to fly;
Behold, with what rapidity
I skip about from place to place,
And still unwearied with the race;
But you—how lazily you creep,
And stop to breathe at every step!
Whenever I your bulk survey,
I pity—"   What he meant to say,
Or with what kind of peroration
He'd have concluded his oration,
I cannot tell; for, all at once,
There pounced upon the learned dunce
An ambushed Cat; who, very soon,
Experimentally made known,
That between Mice and Elephants
There is a mighty difference.

### MORAL.

When fools pretend to wit and sense,
And wish to shine at your expense,
Defy them to the proof, and you
Will make them their own folly show.

# FABLE LXXVI.

### THE HUSBANDMAN AND HIS SONS.

A CERTAIN Husbandman, lying at the point of death, and being desirous his sons should pursue that innocent, entertaining course of agriculture in which he himself had been engaged all his life, made use of this expedient to induce them to it. He called them to his bed-side and spoke to this effect: "All the patrimony I have to bequeath you, Sons, is my farm and my vineyard, of which I make you joint heirs. But I charge you not to let it go out of your own occupation; for if I have any treasure besides, it lies buried somewhere in the ground, within a foot of the surface."

This made the Sons conclude that he talked of money which he had hid there; so, after their father's death, with unwearied diligence and application, they carefully dug up every inch, both of the farm and vineyard; from which it came to pass that, though they missed the treasure which they expected, the ground, by being so well stirred and loosened, produced so plentiful a crop of all that was sowed in it as proved a real, and no inconsiderable treasure.

MORAL.

Labour and industry, well applied, seldom fail of finding a rich treasure. And if these do not give us exactly the wealth we are looking for, they will certainly give us health and cheerfulness, with a tranquil mind, and, without these, all the gold of Peru would lie in our coffers useless.

—◦—

## FABLE LXXVII.

### THE BALD KNIGHT.

A CERTAIN Knight growing old, his hair fell off, and he became bald; to hide which imperfection he wore a periwig. But as he was riding out with some others a-hunting, a sudden gust of wind blew off the periwig, and exposed his bald pate.

The company could not forbear laughing at the accident; and he himself laughed as loud as anybody, saying, "How was it to be expected that I should keep strange hair on my head, when my own would not stay there."

MORAL.

If, by any word or action, we happen to raise the laughter of those about us, we cannot stifle it better than, by a brisk presence of mind, to join in the mirth of the company, and, if possible, anticipate the jests they are ready to make on us.

## FABLE LXXVIII.

### THE DOG IN THE MANGER.

A Dog was lying upon a manger full of hay. An Ox, being hungry, came near, and wanted to eat of the hay; but the envious, ill-natured cur, getting up and snarling at him, would not suffer him to touch it. Upon which the Ox, in the bitterness of his heart, said, "What a selfish wretch thou art, for thou canst neither eat hay thyself, nor suffer others to do so."

### MORAL.

Selfishness is a most contemptible thing; but that degree of it which withholds from others what we can make no possible use of ourselves, is hateful in the extreme.

## FABLE LXXIX.

### THE OLD MAN AND DEATH.

A poor, feeble old Man, who had crawled out into a neighbouring wood to gather a few sticks, had made up his bundle,

THE DOG IN THE MANGER.

and, laying it over his shoulders, was trudging homeward with it; but what with age, and the length of the way, and the weight of his burden, he grew so faint and weak that he sunk under it, and, as he sat on the ground, called upon Death to come and ease him of his troubles. Death no sooner heard him than he came and demanded of him what he wanted. The poor old creature, who little thought Death had been so near, and frightened almost out of his senses with his terrible aspect, answered him, trembling, That, having by chance let his bundle of sticks fall, and being too infirm to get it up himself, he had made bold to call upon him to help him; that, indeed, this was all he wanted at present, and that he hoped his worship was not offended with him for the liberty he had taken in so doing.

MORAL.

Men lightly speak of Death when they think he is far away; but let him appear near, and the very sense of his approach almost drives the life away. Men then resume the burden of cares which they had thrown down as insupportable, being content to bear the ills they have than fly to others that they know not of.

## FABLE LXXX.

### THE OLD HEN AND YOUNG COCK.

As an old Hen led forth her train,
And seemed to peck, to show the grain;
She raked the chaff, she scratched the ground,
And gleaned the spacious yard around.
A giddy chick, to try her wings,
On the well's narrow margin springs,
And prone she drops.   The mother's breast
All day with sorrow was possessed.

A Cock she met—her son, she knew;
And in her heart affection grew.

" My son," says she, " I grant, your years
Have reached beyond a mother's cares;
I see you vigorous, strong, and bold;
I hear, with joy, your triumphs told.
'Tis not from Cocks thy fate I dread;
But let thy ever-wary tread
Avoid yon well; that fatal place
Is sure perdition to our race.

Print this, my counsel, on thy breast;
To the just gods I leave the rest."

He thanked her care; yet, day by day,
His bosom burned to disobey;
And every time the well he saw,
Scorned, in his heart, the foolish law;
Near and more near each day he drew,
And longed to try the dangerous view.

"Why was this idle charge?" he cries;
"Let courage female fears despise!
Or did she doubt my heart was brave,
And, therefore, this injunction gave?
Or does her harvest store the place,
A treasure for her younger race?
And would she thus my search prevent?—
I stand resolved, and dare th' event."

Thus said, he mounts the margin's round,
And pries into the depth profound.
He stretched his neck; and, from below,
With stretching neck advanced a foe:
With wrath his ruffled plumes he ears;
The foe with ruffled plumes appears:

Threat answered threat, his fury grew;
Headlong to meet the war he flew;
But when the watery death he found,
He thus lamented as he drowned:
"I ne'er had been in this condition,
Had I obeyed the prohibition."

### MORAL.

Obey your parents, or 'twill be your fate,
To feel repentance when it comes too late.

## FABLE LXXXI.

### MERCURY AND THE WOODMAN.

A MAN was felling a tree on the bank of a river, and by chance let his hatchet slip out of his hand, which dropped into the water, and immediately sunk to the bottom. Being, therefore, in great distress from the loss of his tool, he sat down and bemoaned himself most lamentably.

Upon this, Mercury appeared to him, and being informed of the cause of his complaint, dived to the bottom of the river, and, coming up again, showed the man a golden hatchet, demanding if that were his. He denied that it was;

upon which Mercury dived a second time, and brought up a silver one. The Man refused it, alleging likewise that this was not his. He dived a third time, and fetched up the individual hatchet the man had lost; upon sight of which the poor fellow was overjoyed, and took it with all humility and thankfulness. Mercury was so pleased with the fellow's honesty, that he gave him the other two into the bargain, as a reward for his just dealing.

The man then went to his companions, and, giving them an account of what had happened, one of them went presently to the river side, and let his hatchet fall designedly into the stream. Then, sitting down upon the bank, he fell a-weeping and lamenting, as if he had been really and sorely afflicted. Mercury appeared as before, and, diving, brought him up a golden hatchet, asking if that was the one he had lost. Transported at the precious metal, he answered "Yes," and went to snatch it greedily. But the god, detesting his abominable impudence, not only refused to give him that, but would not so much as let him have his own hatchet again.

### MORAL.

Honesty is the best policy; it has made many a man's fortune, being blessed by God, and highly valued by man.

I

## FABLE LXXXII.

### THE WOLF AND THE KID.

THE Goat, going abroad to feed, shut up her young kid at home, charging him to bolt the door fast, and open it to nobody, till she herself should return. The Wolf, who lay lurking just by, heard this charge given, and soon after came and knocked at the door, counterfeiting the voice of the Goat, and desiring to be admitted. The Kid, looking out of the window and discovering the cheat, bid him go about his business; for however he might imitate a Goat's voice, yet he appeared too much like a Wolf to be trusted.

### MORAL.

We cannot use too much caution in avoiding those things which those who have more experience than we have warned us against.

## FABLE LXXXIII.

### THE OLD MAN AND HIS SONS.

AN Old Man had many Sons, who were often falling out with one another. When the father had exerted his authority,

THE WOLF AND THE GOAT.

and used other means in order to reconcile them, and all to no purpose, he at last had recourse to this expedient: he ordered his Sons to be called before him, and a short bundle of sticks to be brought; and then commanded them, one by one, to try if, with all their might and strength, they could any of them break it. They all tried, but to no purpose; for the sticks being closely and compactly bound up together, it was impossible for the force of man to do it.

After this the father ordered the bundle to be untied, and gave a single stick to each of his Sons, at the same time bidding him try to break it, which, when each did, with all imaginable ease, the father addressed himself to them to this effect: " O, my sons, behold the power of unity! for if you, in like manner, would but keep yourselves strictly joined in the bonds of friendship, it would not be in the power of any mortal to hurt you ; but when once the ties of brotherly affection are dissolved, how soon do you fall to pieces, and become liable to be violated by every injurious hand that assaults you."

### MORAL.

Union is strength. Love is a powerful bond, which, when cherished, will make those who are bound together by it, irresistible.

## FABLE LXXXIV.

### THE BROOK AND THE FOUNTAIN.

A Fountain varied gambols played,
　　Close by an humble Brook;
While gently murmuring through the glade,
　　Its peaceful course it took.

Perhaps it gave one envious gaze
　　Upon the Fountain's height,
While glittering in the morning rays
　　Pre-eminently bright.

In all the colours of the sky,
　　Alternately it shone:
The Brook observed it with a sigh,
　　But quietly rolled on.

The owner of the Fountain died;
　　Neglect soon brought decay;
The bursting pipes were ill-supplied;
　　The Fountain ceased to play.

But still the Brook its peaceful course
   Continued to pursue;
Her ample, inexhausted source,
   From Nature's fount she drew.

"Now," said the Brook, "I bless my fate,
   My showy rival gone;
Contented in its native state
   My little stream rolls on.

And all the world has cause, indeed,
   To own, with grateful heart,
How much great Nature's works excel
   The feeble works of art."

MORAL.

Humble usefulness is preferable to idle splendour.

———o———

## FABLE LXXXV.

### THE MICE IN COUNCIL.

THE Mice called a general council, and, having met, after
the doors were locked, entered into a free consultation about
ways and means how to render their fortunes and estates

more secure from the danger of the Cat. Many things were offered, and much was debated, "pro and con," upon the matter. At last, a young Mouse, in a fine, florid speech, concluded with an expedient, and that the only one, which was to put them for the future entirely out of the power of the enemy; and this was that the Cat should wear a bell about her neck, which, upon the least motion, would give the alarm, and be a signal for them to retire into their holes. This speech was received with great applause, and it was even proposed by some that the Mouse who made it should have the thanks of the assembly; upon which an old, grave Mouse, who had sat silent all the while, stood up, and, in another speech, owned that the contrivance was admirable, and the author of it, without doubt, an ingenious Mouse, but, he said, he thought it would not be so proper to vote him thanks till he should farther inform them how this bell was to be fastened about the Cat's neck, and what Mouse would undertake to do it.

#### MORAL.

Many things appear excellent in theory which are impossible in practice. It often requires a great deal of courage to carry out projects which a fine, florid speech may persuade the hearers are most plausible.

## FABLE LXXXVI.

### THE FOX IN THE WELL.

A Fox, having fallen into a well, made a shift by sticking his claws into the sides to keep his head above water. Soon after a Wolf came and peeped over the brink, to whom the Fox applied very earnestly for assistance; entreating that he would help him to a rope, or something of the kind, which might favour his escape. The Wolf moved with compassion at his misfortune, could not forbear expressing his concern. "Ah, poor Reynard," says he, "I am sorry for you with all my heart; how could you possibly come into this melancholy condition?"

"Nay, pr'ythee, friend," replied the Fox, "if you wish me well, do not stand pitying me, but lend me some succour as fast as you can; for pity is but cold comfort when one is up to the chin in water, and within a hair's breadth of starving or drowning.

#### MORAL.

Mere expressions of pity, without a desire or attempt to alleviate suffering, are a mockery. He that would be truly a friend, will be ready to give his assistance when needed.

## FABLE LXXXVIII.

### THE HORSE AND THE WOLF.

As a Wolf was roaming over a farm, he came to a field of oats, but not being able to eat them, he left them and went his way,

Presently, meeting with a Horse, he bade him come with him into the field, " For," says he, " I have found some capital oats; and I have not tasted one, but have kept them all for you, for the very sound of your teeth is music to my ear." But the Horse replied, " A pretty fellow! if Wolves were able to eat oats, I suspect you would not have preferred your ears to your appetite."

### MORAL.

Little thanks are due to him, who only gives away whatever is of no use to himself.

———o———

## FABLE LXXXIX.

### THE TWO SPRINGS.

Two springs, which issued from the same mountain, began their course together : one of them took her way in a silent

THE HORSE AND THE WOLF.

and gentle stream, while the other rushed along with a
sounding and rapid current. " Sister," said the latter, "at
the rate you move, you will probably be dried up, before you
advance much farther; whereas, for myself, I will venture a
wager, that, within two or three hundred furlongs, I shall
become navigable; and, after distributing commerce and
wealth wherever I flow, I shall majestically proceed to pay
my tribute to the ocean. So, farewell, dear sister! and
patiently submit to your fate."

Her sister made no reply; but, calmly descending to the
meadows below, increased her stream by numberless little
rills which she collected in her progress, till, at length, she
was enabled to rise into a considerable river; whilst the proud
stream, who had the vanity to depend solely upon her own
sufficiency, continued a shallow brook; and was glad, at last,
to be helped forward, by throwing herself into the arms of
her despised sister.

### MORAL.

His strength in words the blusterer vainly spends,
While steadiness in quiet gains its ends.

# FABLE XC.

### THE COUNTRYMAN AND THE RAVEN.

A RAVEN, while with glossy breast,
Her new laid eggs she fondly pressed,
And, on her wicker-work high mounted,
Her chickens prematurely counted.
(A fault philosophers might blame,
If quite exempted from the same,)
Enjoyed at ease the genial day;
'Twas April, as the bumpkins say;—
The legislature called it May;
But suddenly, a wind, as high
As ever swept a winter's sky,
Shook the young leaves about her ears,
And filled her with a thousand fears,
Lest the rude blast should snap the bough,
And spread her golden hopes below.
But just at eve the blowing weather,
And all her fears, were hushed together.
"And now, quoth poor unthinking Ralph,
"'Tis over, and the brood is safe."

(For Ravens, though as birds of omen,
They teach both conjurors and old women;
To tell us what is to befall,
Can't prophesy themselves at all.)
The morning came, when neighbour Hodge,
Who long had marked her airy lodge,
And destined all the treasure there,
A gift to his expecting fair,
Climbed, like a squirrel to his dray,
And bore the worthless prize away.

### MORAL.

Safety consists not in escape
From danger of a frightful shape;
Fate steals along with silent tread,
Found oftenest in what least we dread;
Frowns in the storm with angry brow,
But in the sunshine strikes the blow.

---

# FABLE XCI.

### THE FOX AND THE BRAMBLE.

A Fox, hard pressed by the hounds, was getting over a
hedge, but tore his foot upon a Bramble, which grew just in

the midst of it, upon which he reproached the Bramble for his inhospitable cruelty in using a stranger, which had fled to him for protection, after such a barbarous manner. "Yes," says the Bramble, "you intended to have made me serve your turn, I know; but take this piece of advice with you for the future: Never lay hold of a Bramble again, as you value your sweet person; for laying hold is a privilege that belongs to us Brambles, and we do not care to let it go out of the family."

### MORAL.

Impertinent people, who take liberties with others, are often much surprised if they are retorted on with severity. It is better, then, to keep from undue familiarity with strangers, for we know not of what temper they may be.

———o———

## FABLE XCII.

### HERCULES AND THE CARTER.

As a clownish fellow was driving his cart along a deep miry lane, the wheels stuck so fast in the clay, that the horses could not draw them out. Upon this he fell a-bawling and praying to Hercules to come and help him.

Hercules, looking down from a cloud, bade him not lie

there, like an idle rascal, as he was, but get up and whip his horses stoutly, and clap his shoulder to the wheel; adding, that this was the only way for him to obtain his assistance.

### MORAL.

The man who asks Heaven for gifts, and neglects the gifts Heaven has given, must expect silence until he shows that he is in earnest by putting his shoulder to the wheel.

——o——

## FABLE XCIII.

### THE BOYS AND THE FROGS.

On the margin of a large lake, which was inhabited by a great number of Frogs, a company of Boys happened to be at play. Their diversion was duck and drake, and whole volleys of stones were thrown into the water, to the great annoyance and danger of the poor terrified Frogs. At length, one of the most hardy, lifting up his head above the surface of the lake;—"Ah! dear children!" said he, "why will ye learn so soon to be cruel? Consider, I beseech you, that though this may be sport to *you*, it is death to *us*."

### MORAL.

A noble mind disdains to gain
Its pleasure from another's pain.

## FABLE XCIV.

### THE COCK AND THE JEWEL.

A BRISK young Cock, in company with two or three pullets, raking upon a dunghill for something to entertain them with, happened to scratch up a jewel, which sparkled with an exceeding bright lustre; but, not knowing what to do with it, endeavoured to cover his ignorance under a look of contempt. So, shrugging up his wings, shaking his head, and putting on a grimace, he expressed himself to this purpose: "Indeed, you are a very fine thing, but I know not what business you have here. I make no scruple of declaring that my taste lies quite another way, and I had rather have one grain of dear delicious barley than all the jewels under the sun."

### MORAL.

We should not despise as worthless what does not come within the limit of our understanding. Some lose what is truly valuable for want of knowledge, and prefer what is comparatively worthless.

THE COCK AND THE JEWEL.

## FABLE XCV.

### THE NIGHTINGALE AND THE GLOW-WORM.

A NIGHTINGALE, that, all day long,
Had cheered the village with his song,
Nor yet at eve his note suspended,
Nor yet when eventide was ended,
Began to feel, as well he might,
The keen demands of appetite;
When, looking eagerly around,
He spied, far off, upon the ground,
A something shining in the dark,
And knew the Glow-worm by his spark;
So, stooping down from hawthorn top,
He thought to put him in his crop.
The Worm, aware of his intent,
Harangued him thus, right eloquent:—
"Did you admire my lamp," quoth he,
"As much as I your minstrelsy,
You would abhor to do me wrong,
As much as I to spoil your song;
For 'twas the self-same power divine
Taught you to sing and me to shine;

That you with music, I with light,
Might beautify and cheer the night."
The songster heard his short oration,
And, warbling out his approbation,
Released him, as my story tells,
And found a supper somewhere else.


### MORAL.

From this short fable, youth may learn
Their real interest to discern,
That brother should not strive with brother,
And worry and oppress each other;
But, joined in unity and peace,
Their mutual happiness increase:
Pleased when each others' faults they hide,
And in their virtues feel a pride.

—o—

## FABLE XCVI.

### THE FOX AND THE SICK LION.

It was reported that the Lion was sick, and the beasts were made to believe that they could not make their court better than by going to visit him. Upon this, they generally went, but it was particularly remarked that the Fox was not one of the number. The Lion, therefore, dispatched one of his Jackals to sound him about it, and to ask him why he had so little charity and respect as never to come near him at a time when he lay so dangerously ill, and everybody else had been to see him. "Why," replied the Fox, "pray present my duty to his majesty, and tell him that I have the same respect for him as ever, and have been coming several times to kiss his royal paw, but I am so terribly frightened at the mouth of his cave, to see the print of my fellow-subjects' feet all pointing forwards, and none backwards, that I had not resolution enough to venture in."

Now, the truth of the matter was, that the sickness of the Lion was only a sham to draw the beasts into his den, the more easily to devour them.

### MORAL.

It is well to weigh and consider the nature of any proposal thoroughly before we accede to it; but, certainly, if we have reason, from the injury done to others, to suspect that we may suffer harm, it is decidedly better to decline.

K

## FABLE XCVI.

### THE LION, THE FOX, AND THE GEESE.

A LION, tired with state affairs,
Quite sick of pomp, and worn with cares,
Resolved (remote from noise and strife)
In peace to pass his latter life.

It was proclaimed : the day was set :
Behold the general council met :
The Fox was viceroy named.   The crowd
To the new regent humbly bowed !
Wolves, bears, and mighty tigers bend,
And strive who most shall condescend.
The crowd admire his wit, his sense :
Each word hath weight and consequence.
The flatterer all his art displays ;
He who hath power, is sure of praise.
A Fox stepped forth before the rest,
And thus the servile throng addressed :—

" How vast his talents, born to rule,
And train'd in virtue's honest school !

What clemency his temper sways !
How uncorrupt are all his ways !
Beneath his conduct and command
Rapine shall cease to waste the land ;
What blessings must attend the nation
Under this good administration !"

He said.   A Goose, who distant stood,
Harangu'd apart the cackling brood :

"Whene'er I hear a knave commend,
He bids me shun his worthy friend.
What praise ! what mighty commendation !
But 'twas a Fox who spoke th' oration.
Foxes this government may prize,
As gentle, plentiful, and wise ;
If they enjoy the sweets, 'tis plain
We Geese must feel a tyrant reign.
What havoc now shall thin our race !
When every petty clerk in place,
To prove his taste, and seem polite,
Will feed on Geese both noon and night."

### MORAL.

Those flatter the plunderer who share in the spoil.

# FABLE XCVII.

## THE ONE-EYED DOE.

A Doe, that had but one eye, used to graze near the sea, and that she might be the more secure from harm, she kept her blind side toward the water, from whence she had no apprehension of danger, and with the other surveyed the country as she fed.

By this vigilance and precaution she thought herself in the utmost security; when a sly fellow, with two or three of his companions, who had been poaching after her several days to no purpose, at last took a boat, and, fetching a compass upon the sea, came gently down upon her, and shot her. The Doe, in the agonies of death, breathed out this doleful complaint :—" Oh, hard fate! that I should receive my death wound from that side whence I expected no ill; and be safe in that part where I looked for the most danger."

### MORAL.

Our troubles and dangers frequently arise from the direction we least expect them.

THE ONE-EYED DOE.

## FABLE XCVIII.

### THE FOX, THE RAVEN, AND THE DOVE.

A Fox, who was half-starved with hunger, stretched himself all along upon the ground, and lay as if he were dead, that he might entice the harmless birds to come within his reach, and then leap of a sudden upon them, and make them his prey; but it happened that a Raven, who was hovering near him, observed that he fetched his breath; and, by consequence, found it to be only a trick in him to catch the birds. She, therefore, instantly gave them notice of it; and forewarned them, as they valued their own lives, not to come within reach of the Fox, who only feigned himself to be dead.

The Fox, finding his plot to be discovered, was obliged to go away hungry; but soon bethought himself of another invention: which was, to go and kennel himself in a hollow tree, upon which a Dove had her nest, and was breeding up her young ones. Having done this, he called to her, that, unless she would throw down to him sometimes one of her eggs, and sometimes one of her young ones, he would climb up the tree, take away all her eggs, kill both her and her young, and break her nest to pieces.

The harmless Dove, thinking of two ills to choose the

least, did as the Fox required her; and threw him down now
one of her eggs, and then one of her young ones. Having
done so, for some time, with a great deal of grief and sorrow,
and the Fox continuing still to demand it of her, she, at last,
made her complaint to the Raven, who chanced to come and
perch herself on the same tree; grievously bemoaning her
fate, that she, like a good mother, to provide for her children,
was at last obliged to make them a sacrifice to such a villain.
But the Raven, who was not so timorous as she, advised her,
whenever the Fox threatened her again, that he would kill
both her and her young, if she would not throw one of them
down to him, to answer him roundly,—"If you could have
flown or climbed up the tree, you would not have been so
often contented with one of my eggs, or of my young; but
would, long since, according to your ravenous and blood-
thirsty nature, have devoured both me and them." In short,
the next time the Fox came, and threatened her as before,
she replied as the Raven had instructed her.

The Fox, hearing her answer, and knowing very well that
she was not so wise and cunning of herself, resolved to find
out the truth of the matter; and, at length, came to under-
stand that it was the Raven who had been her counsellor.
He, therefore, vowed to be revenged on her, who had now,
the second time, hindered him from getting his prey. Not
long after, he espied her sitting on a high thorn-tree; and,
going to her, began to praise her at a mighty rate,—

magnifying her good fortune above that of all beasts, who could neither fly like her, nor tread the ground with so majestical a gait: adding, withal, that it would be a great pleasure to him to see her lordly walk; that he might from thence, be certain whether she were indeed so divine and prophetic a bird as men had always held her to be.

The Raven, transported to hear herself thus praised to the skies, flew down; and, pitching upon the ground, walked to and fro, in mighty pomp and state. The Fox seemed highly delighted; and said, that he extremely wondered how the Raven could keep upon the ground, when the wind blew her feathers over her eyes, and hindered her sight; but chiefly when it blew before, behind, and on all sides of her. "I can very well provide against that," said the Raven; "for then I hide my head under my left wing." "How!" cried the Fox; "hide your head under your left wing! So wonderful a thing I can never believe, till I see it." Immediately the Raven put her head under her left wing, and held it there so long that the Fox caught hold of her and killed her for his prey.

#### MORAL.

·So must they fare who give good advice to others, but have not discretion enough to follow it themselves.

## FABLE XCIX.

### THE TWO POTS.

Two Pots, of different size and matter made,
Were swiftly down a rolling stream convey'd.
The larger vessel, form'd of solid brass,
Did boldly o'er the rapid water pass;
While that whose substance was but brittle clay,
Would, for his safety, give the stronger way.
Him the Brass Pot invited to draw near,
And said, " His frailty need not cause his fear;
For he, with just precaution would prevent
The danger of their jostling as they went."
  The Earthen Pot, that knew his weaker frame,
Excused himself, that he no nearer came;
And said, " My friend, if the impetuous tide
Should dash my clay against your brazen side,
By the hard fate of that unequal stroke,
While you are whole, I shall be surely broke."

### MORAL.

Men safest still in equal friendship live,
Where they can do no harm, and none receive:

The strong, by power led to insult the weak,
With every touch the brittle vessels break;
While they, abused and injured by the strong,
Must, without remedy, sustain the wrong.

—o—

## FABLE C.

### THE TWO FROGS.

ONE hot, sultry summer, the lakes and ponds being almost everywhere dried up, a couple of Frogs agreed to travel together in search of water. At last they came to a deep well, and, sitting on the brink of it, began to consult whether they should leap in or no. One of them was so inclined, urging that there was plenty of clear, spring water, and no danger of being disturbed. "Well," says the other, "all this may be true, and yet I cannot come into your opinion for my life; for if the water should happen to dry up here too, how should we get out again."

### MORAL.

Skilful generals always secure a way for retreat. "Look before you leap" is an old and trite proverb. We should not undertake any action of importance without considering what may be the result, in all its aspects.

## FABLE CI.

### THE FOX AND THE MASK.

A Fox, being in a shop where Masks were sold, laid his foot upon one of them, and considering it awhile attentively, at last broke out into this exclamation :—"Bless me!" says he, "what a handsome face this is! What a pity it is that it should want brains!"

#### MORAL.

Beauty without sense is of little value. A fair outside is but a poor substitute for inward worth.

——o——

## FABLE CII.

### THE CAT, THE COCK, AND THE YOUNG MOUSE.

A Young Mouse, that had seen very little of the world, came running, one day, to his mother in great haste:—"Oh, mother!" said he, "I am frightened almost to death! I have seen the most extraordinary creature that ever was. He has a fierce, angry look, and struts about on two legs; a strange piece of flesh grows on his head, and another under his throat, as red as blood: he flapped his arms against his sides, as if he intended to rise into the air; and stretching out his

THE FOX AND THE MASK.

head, he opened a sharp-pointed mouth so wide, that I thought he was preparing to swallow me up: then he roared at me so horribly, that I trembled in every joint, and was glad to run home as fast as I could. If I had not been frightened away by this terrible monster, I was just going to commence an acquaintance with the prettiest creature you ever saw. She had a soft fur skin, thicker than ours, and all beautifully streaked with black and grey; with a modest look, and a demeanour so humble and courteous, that methought I could have fallen in love with her. Then she had a fine, long tail, which she waved about so prettily, and looked so earnestly at me, that I do believe she was just going to speak to me, when the horrid monster frightened me away."

"Ah, my dear child!" said the mother, "you have escaped being devoured, but not by that monster you were so much afraid of; which, in truth, was only a bird, and would have done you no manner of harm. Whereas, the sweet creature, of whom you seem so fond, was no other than a Cat; who, under that hypocritical countenance, conceals the most inveterate hatred to all our race, and subsists entirely by devouring Mice. Learn from this incident, my dear, never, while you live, to rely on outward appearances."

## MORAL.

Beneath a fair, alluring guise,
A hidden danger often lies.

## FABLE CIII.

### THE MICE AND THE TRAP.

ONCE upon a time, the Mice saw a broiled rasher of bacon hanging up in a very little room, the door of which being open, enticed them to fall on with greedy appetites. But some of them took particular notice that there was but one way into the room, and, by consequence, but one way to get out of it; so that, if that door, by misfortune or art, should chance to be shut, they would all be inevitably taken: they could not, therefore, find in their hearts to venture in; but said, that they had rather content themselves with homely fare, in safety, than, for the sake of a dainty bit, to run the danger of being taken, and lost for ever.

The other Mice, who were looked upon to be great epicures, declared that they saw no danger; and, therefore, ran into the room, and fell to eating the bacon with great delight: but they soon heard the door fall down, and saw that they were all taken. Then the fear of approaching death so seized them, that they found no relish in their exquisite food; and immediately came the Cook who had set the Trap, and killed them: but the others, who had contented themselves with their usual food, fled into their holes, and, by that means, preserved their lives.

# FABLE CIV.

## THE CHAMELEON.

OFT has it been my lot to mark
A proud, conceited, talking spark,
With eyes that hardly served at most
To guard their master 'gainst a post;
Yet round the world the blade has been,
To see whatever could be seen.
Returning from his finish'd tour,
Grown ten times perter than before,
Whatever word you chance to drop,
The travelled fool your mouth will stop;
" Sir, if my judgment you'll allow,—
I've seen,—and, sure, I ought to know;"—
So begs you'd pay a due submission,
And acquiesce in his decision.

Two travellers, of such a cast,
As o'er Arabia's wilds they pass'd,

And on their way, in friendly chat,
Now talked of this, and then of that;
Discoursed awhile, 'mongst other matter,
Of the Chameleon's form and nature.
"A stranger animal," cries one,
"Sure never lived beneath the sun:
A lizard's body, lean and long,
A fish's head, a serpent's tongue.
In truth, with triple jaw disjoin'd;
And what a length of tail behind!
How slow its pace! and then its hue!
Who ever saw so fine a blue?"


"Hold there!" the other quick replies,
"'Tis green:—I saw it with these eyes,
As late with open mouth it lay,
And warm'd it in the sunny ray:
Stretch'd at its ease the beast I view'd,
And saw it eat the air for food."


"I've seen it, sir, as well as you,
And must again affirm it blue;
At leisure I the beast survey'd,
Extended in the cooling shade."

" ' Tis green ! 'tis green ! sir, I assure ye."—
" Green !" cries the other, in a fury,—
" Why, sir, d'ye think I've lost my eyes ? "
" ' Twere no great loss ! " the friend replies ;
" For if they always serve you thus,
You find 'em but of little use."


So high at last the contest rose,
From words they almost came to blows ;
When, luckily, came by a third ;
To him the question they referr'd ;
And begged he'd tell 'em, if he knew,
Whether the thing was green or blue.


" Sirs," cries the umpire, " cease your pother—
The creature's neither one nor t'other.
I caught the animal last night,
And viewed it o'er by candle-light ;
I marked it well—'twas black as jet ;—
You stare—but, sirs, I've got it yet,
And can produce it."—" Pray, sir, do ;
I'll lay my life the thing is blue."
" And I'll be sworn that when you've seen
The reptile, you'll pronounce him green."

" Well, then, at once to ease the doubt,"
Replies the man, " I'll turn him out;
And when before your eyes I've set him,
If you don't find him black I'll eat him;"
He said. Then full before their sight,
Produced the beast, and lo! 'twas white.
Both stared, the man looked wondrous wise.
" My children," the Chameleon cries,
(Then first the creature found a tongue),
" You all are right and all are wrong;
When next you talk of what you view,
Think others see as well as you;
Nor wonder, if you find that none
Prefers your eye-sight to his own."

———o———

## FABLE CV.

### THE WOLF, THE FOX, AND THE ASS.

THE Lion, as king of the beasts, made a law that no
beast should, without lawful cause, do any hurt to another;
and should come once a year to court, to confess, and be
absolved or punished, according to his deserts. Now it
happened that the Wolf and the Fox were going thither

together, and overtaking the Ass on the road, said to him:—
"Brother, it is a long way to court, and it certainly must be
much more tedious to you than to ourselves, because of your
slow pace; but we can avoid the trouble of going thither, if
you think fit. Let us three confess ourselves to one another,
and send our absolutions to court, attested by two of us as
witnesses."

The Ass liked the proposal; into a clover field they
went, and the Fox thus confessed himself first:—"It happened, as I was going one night through a village, a Cock, by
his loud crowing, disturbed all the people that were asleep; at
which I grew very angry, and bit off his head; then, fearing
that the stench of his dead body might be offensive to the
Hens, I ate him up. Nevertheless, it happened, three days
after, as I was going by the same village, those very Hens
spied me; and, instead of thanking me for the great kindness
I had done them, cried out, 'Murderer, murderer!' Then
I, in defence of my honour, killed three of them; and, lest
they should have stunk and offended the neighbourhood, ate
them up too. This is all I have done; for which I now
await your sentence."

The Wolf thereupon expressed himself thus:—"You
have, indeed, offended against the letter of our monarch's
law, but not against the meaning of it; since your intentions
were honourable, to take care of the quiet of men, and to

vindicate your injured reputation. If, therefore, you will promise never to be so hasty again in killing any beast, I vote for your absolution." This the Fox readily did; and the Ass joined in opinion with the Wolf, who then thus began his confession :—

"As I was one day walking along, I saw a Sow trampling down the corn of a poor peasant, and tearing it up by the roots, while her hungry Pigs were strayed far from her, and could not get themselves out of the mire; so that I, growing very angry at the great mischief she did the peasant, and at her neglect of motherly duty, killed and ate her up. Three days after, chancing to go again the same way, I observed that those Pigs were grown very lean ; and reflecting that, through want of their mother's milk, they would certainly die a languishing death, I put an end to their miseries, and ate them up too. This I have to confess."

The Fox instantly argued in this manner:—" Though you confess to having killed both mother and children; and though it seems, at first sight, that you have heinously offended against the law of our king; yet I see, nevertheless, that your intentions were good : to prevent mischief from falling upon men, to stir up a mother to her duty, and to show compassion to her miserable children, are virtues that no law can forbid or punish. I, therefore, declare you absolved." To which the Ass agreed.

The Ass then made his confession:—"You both know," said he, "that it is not in my nature to do hurt to other beasts, nor to shed blood; and, therefore, you cannot expect to hear any such thing from me; but, to content you, I will relate to you what happened innocently to me, while I was in the service of a master. He was an old man, and apt to take cold in his feet; so that, when he travelled, to keep them dry and warm, he was wont to stick a little hay in his shoes. Now I carried him, one winter, to an inn, where he was to lie all night; and when we came to the door, the innkeeper brought him a pair of dry slippers, that his dirty shoes might not soil the house; so that he pulled them off, and left them without, and me by them. In short, my master and his host found themselves so well in the chimney-corner, that they never thought of poor me; but left me all night in the bitter cold, without giving me a handful of food: so that I ate up all the hay that stuck in his shoes. This is all I have to say; —if you will call it a confession, you may: however, I think nothing can be said against it."

"Oh!" said the Fox, immediately, "this is not, indeed, an offence against the letter of the law, which mentions only the doing hurt to beasts, and takes no notice of eating of hay; but, if we reflect on the dangerous consequences of this action, and that so reverend a creature as a chill, aged man, by being thus robbed of his hay in the winter, and the next day continuing his road without it, might have caught a cold, a cough, and a cholic, that would have brought his grey hairs to the grave:—whoever, I say, reflects on this, cannot but be of my opinion,—which is, that the Ass largely deserves to die. Cousin Wolf, what say you to this matter?" "I," said the Wolf, "am of opinion that by reason of the ill consequences that might have attended this action, the Ass deserves a double death, and to be made an example to others." With that he leaped upon him, and tore out his throat, and the Fox and he immediately ate him up.

MORAL.

Knaves can always find reasons for justifying their own conduct, and condemning that of others.

———o———

FABLE CVI.

THE BOY AND THE BUTTERFLY.

A BOY, greatly smitten with the colours of a Butterfly, pursued it from flower to flower with indefatigable pains. First, he aimed to surprise it among the leaves of a rose; then to cover it with his hat, as it was feeding on a daisy; now hoped to secure it, as it rested on a sprig of myrtle;

and now grew sure of his prize, perceiving it loiter on a bed of violets. But the fickle Fly, continually changing one blossom for another, still eluded his attempts. At length, observing it half buried in the cup of a tulip, he rushed forward, and snatching it with violence, crushed it all to pieces.

MORAL.

Pleasure, like the Butterfly,
Will still elude as we draw nigh;
And when we think we hold it fast,
Will, like the insect, breathe its last.

———o———

## FABLE CVII.

### THE CROW AND THE PITCHER.

A CROW, ready to die with thirst, flew with joy to a Pitcher, which he beheld at some distance. When he came he found water in it, indeed, but so near the bottom that, with all his stooping and straining, he was not able to reach it. Then he endeavoured to overturn the Pitcher, that so at least he might be able to get a little of it. But his strength was not sufficient for this. At last, seeing some pebbles lie near the place, he cast them one by one into the Pitcher;

and thus, by degrees, raised the water up to the very brim, and satisfied his thirst.

MORAL.

Necessity is the mother of invention, and that which cannot be accomplished by strength may be achieved by ingenuity.

WHERE THERE IS A WILL. THERE IS A WAY.

WERTHEIMER, LEA AND CO. PRINTERS, FINSBURY CIRCUS.

# GRIFFITH & FARRAN'S NEW AND POPULAR WORKS FOR THE YOUNG.

---

**THE HISTORY OF THE ROBINS.** By Mrs. TRIMMER. A New Edition, with Twenty-four beautiful Illustrations from Drawings by HARRISON WEIR. Small 4to, price 6s. extra cloth ; 7s. 6d. cloth elegant, gilt edges.

"The delicious story of Dicksy, Flapsy and Picksey—who can have forgotten it? Harrison Weir is the Painter Laureate of the lower world, we have, therefore, a most attractive book."—*Art Journal.*

**THE LITTLE GIPSY.** By ÉLIE SAUVAGE. Translated by ANNA BLACKWELL. Profusely Illustrated by LORENZ FRÖLICH. Small 4to, price 5s. cloth ; 6s. cloth elegant, gilt edges.

"An exquisite story, narrated with a grace and charm that will fascinate all readers, young or old. The illustrations are singularly graceful."—*Athenæum.*

**JOHN DEANE OF NOTTINGHAM ; HIS ADVENTURES AND EXPLOITS.** By W. H. G. KINGSTON. With Illustrations. Post 8vo, price 5s. cloth elegant.

**FROM PEASANT TO PRINCE ; OR, THE LIFE OF ALEXANDER PRINCE MENSCHIKOFF.** Freely translated from the Russian by MADAME PIETZKER. With Illustrations. Fcap. 8vo, 2s. 6d. cloth ; 3s. gilt edges.

**MILLICENT AND HER COUSINS.** By the HONORABLE. AUGUSTA BETHELL. With Illustrations. Post 8vo, 3s. 6d. cloth ; 4s. gilt edges.

**BERTRAND DU GUESCLIN, THE HERO OF BRITTANY, CONSTABLE OF FRANCE AND OF CASTILE.** By EMILE DE BONNECHOSE. Translated by MARGARET S. JEUNE. Fcap. 8vo, price 2s. 6d. cloth ; 3s. gilt edges.

**THEODORA : A TALE FOR GIRLS.** By EMILIA MARRYAT NORRIS, Illustrations by GEORGE HAY. Post 8vo, price 4s. 6d. cloth elegant ; 5s. gilt edges.

**ROSAMOND FANE ; OR, THE PRISONERS OF ST. JAMES.** By M. & C. LEE. Illustrations by ROBERT DUDLEY. Post 8vo, price 3s. 6d. cloth elegant ; 4s. gilt edges.

**AMY'S WISH, AND WHAT CAME OF IT.** By Mrs. G. TYLEE. Illustrated by W. WIEGAND. Price 2s. 6d. cloth ; 3s. 6d. coloured, gilt edges.

**TALES OF THE WHITE COCKADE.** By BARBARA HUTTON. With Illustrations by J. LAWSON. Post 8vo, price 5s. cloth ; 5s. 6d. gilt edges.

By the same Author,

**HEROES OF THE CRUSADES.** Illustrations by P. PRIOLO. Post 8vo, price 5s. cloth ; 5s. 6d. gilt edges.

**CASTLES AND THEIR HEROES.** With Illustrations by G. BOWERS. Post 8vo, price 4s. 6d. cloth ; 5s. gilt edges.

---

**TALES OF THE TOYS TOLD BY THEMSELVES.** By FRANCES FREELING BRODERIP. Illustrated by her Brother TOM HOOD. Super-royal 16mo, price 3s. 6d. cloth ; 4s. 6d. coloured, gilt edges.

**THE ADVENTURES OF HANS STERK, THE SOUTH AFRICAN HUNTER AND PIONEER.** By Captain DRAYSON, R.E. With Illustrations by ZWECKER. Post 8vo, price 5s. cloth ; 5s. 6d. gilt edges.

**NEPTUNE ; OR, THE AUTOBIOGRAPHY OF A NEWFOUNDLAND DOG.** By the Author of "Tuppy," etc. With Illustrations by ELWES. Super-royal 16mo, price 2s. 6d. cloth ; 3s. 6d. coloured, gilt edges.

**OUR WHITE VIOLET.** By KAY SPEN, Author of "Gerty and May.'
With Illustrations by T. S. WALE. Super-royal 16mo, price 2s. 6d. cloth; 3s. 6d.
coloured, gilt edges.

**CONSTANCE AND NELLIE; OR, THE LOST WILL.** By EMMA
DAVENPORT. Fcap. 8vo, price 2s. 6d. cloth; 3s. gilt edges.

**THE STOLEN CHERRIES; OR, TELL THE TRUTH AT ONCE.** By
EMILIA MARRYAT NORRIS, daughter of the late CAPTAIN MARRYAT. With
Illustrations by FRASER. Price 2s. 6d. cloth; 3s. 6d. coloured, gilt edges.

**CORNER COTTAGE AND ITS INMATES; OR, TRUST IN GOD.** By
FRANCES OSBORNE. The Illustrations by the Author. Fcap. 8vo, price 2s. 6d.
cloth; 3s. gilt edges.

**THE ATTRACTIVE PICTURE-BOOK:** a New Gift from the Old
Corner. Containing numerous Illustrations by eminent Artists. Super-royal 4to, price
3s. 6d. plain; 7s. 6d. coloured; 10s. 6d. mounted on cloth and coloured, bound in an
elegant cover printed in gold and colours.

**THE BEAR KING:** a Narrative confided to the Marines. By JAMES
GREENWOOD. With Illustrations by ERNEST GRISET. Small 4to, printed on
toned paper. Price 3s. 6d. cloth; 5s. coloured, gilt edges.

**THE BOOK OF CATS:** a Chit-chat Chronicle of Feline Facts and
Fancies. By CHARLES H. ROSS. With Twenty Illustrations by the Author.
Post 8vo, price 4s. 6d. cloth; 5s. gilt edges.

**GERALD AND HARRY; OR, THE BEARS IN THE NORTH.** By EMILIA
MARRYAT NORRIS, Author of "The Early Start in Life," etc. With Six Illustrations by J. B. ZWECKER. Post 8vo, price 5s. cloth; 5s. 6d. gilt edges.

**COUSIN TRIX AND HER WELCOME TALES.** By GEORGINA
M. CRAIK, Author of "Playroom Stories," etc. With Illustrations by F. W. KEYL.
Super-royal 16mo, price 3s. 6d. cloth; 4s. 6d. coloured, gilt edges.

**THE YOUNG VOCALIST:** a Collection of Twelve Songs, each with an
Accompaniment for the Pianoforte, selected from Mozart, Weber, Mendelssohn, Spohr,
etc. By MRS. MOUNSEY BARTHOLOMEW, Associate of the Philharmonic
Society. 4to, price 2s. paper cloth; or 3s. 6d. extra cloth, gilt edges.

"These Lyrics are selected and composed for children who are too young to sing operatic or romantic songs,
or too old for those founded on nursery tales. The melodies are all of a suitable compass, so that the voices
may not be injured by practice at an early age."—*Extract from Preface.*

**CASIMIR, THE LITTLE EXILE.** By CAROLINE PEACHY. With
Illustrations by C. STANTON. Post 8vo, price 4s. 6d. cloth elegant.

**LUCY'S CAMPAIGN:** a Story of Adventure. By MARY and CATHE-
RINE LEE. With Illustrations by GEORGE HAY. Fcap. 8vo, price 3s. cloth elegant
3s. 6d. gilt edges.

"Written with some of the grace and facility that distinguish the literary style of the two sisters—Sophia
and Harriet Lee."—*Athenæum.*

**HELEN IN SWITZERLAND.** By the HON. AUGUSTA BETHELL,
Author of "The Echoes of an Old Bell." With Illustrations by E. WHYMPER.
Super-royal 16mo, price 3s. 6d. cloth extra; 4s. 6d. coloured, gilt edges.

*\*\* A Complete Catalogue of G. & F.'s Publications sent post free on
application.*

www.ingramcontent.com/pod-product-compliance
Lightning Source LLC
Chambersburg PA
CBHW030831270326
41928CB00007B/1000